A complete Guide to maximum energy savings in a domestic household

C. B. Hotnoga TMIET AEE BESA

A complete Guide to maximum energy savings in a domestic household

Cambridge, United Kingdom

2020 Edition

Save BIG on your energy and water bills.

Any household can lead exactly the same lifestyles whilst cutting down at least 25% on energy and water expenses, and helping the Environment at the same time.

By C. B. Hotnoga TMIET AEE BESA

Institution of Engineering and Technology

Association of Energy Engineers

Building and Engineering Services Association

1

C. B. Hotnoga TMIET AEE BESA

A complete Guide to maximum energy savings in a domestic household

A complete Guide to maximum energy (electricity and gas) + water savings in a domestic household

Part of Project "CHALLENGE" For the Future

A better approach to energy savings

Greener behaviours in modern day lifestyles

Planning, ahead of changing

Cutting down on natural resources used

Reducing pollution

Fighting climate change

Making BIG SAVINGS on that energy bill

Project "CHALLENGE" includes:

Domestic households

Small sized commercial premises

Medium commercial businesses

Medium and large commercial businesses

with high energy demands

Industrial premises

C. B. Hotnoga TMIET AEE BESA

A complete Guide to maximum energy savings in a domestic household

Contents:

C. B. Hotnoga TMIET AEE BESA

A complete Guide to maximum energy savings in a domestic household

Lighting your property

Indoor lighting

External lighting

Type of light fittings and bulbs

Special lighting, Security, Christmas/Holiday lights, etc.

Live smart not to live in the dark

Ring circuits/Sockets and device charging points

Mobile devices charge points

TVs, computers and other screens

Fridge freezers and electric cookers

Washing machines and tumble dryers

Dishwashers and other high energy consumers

Cold/Hot water dispensing units

Always mindful of what you plug into a socket

C. B. Hotnoga TMIET AEE BESA

A complete Guide to maximum energy savings in a domestic household

Big consumer units with special requirements or protection

Hot tubs and other leisure domestic outlets

Garden electrical tools

Garage and workshop electrical units

Electrical vehicle charging points

Electrical outlets/Big consumer units to avoid

Electric radiators, heating fans

Old/dated appliances

Machines and units not fit for purpose

Appliances not to be used in a domestic environment

Consumer units that will trip or damage domestic electrical installations

Heating up your home

Smart thermostats

Electric heating systems

Electric boilers

Water heaters

Shower heaters

Tap heaters

C. B. Hotnoga TMIET AEE BESA

A complete Guide to maximum energy savings in a domestic household

Cooling your home

Air conditioning

Portable air conditioning units

Fixed and mobile ventilation fans

Efficient cooling ideas that work

Cooling units that make no real difference

Extraction and ventilation units

Kitchen extractor fans

Toilet and shower extraction and ventilation

Humidifiers and dehumidifiers

Air quality without expense

Miscellaneous electrical consumers

Odd consumer units

Big consumers intended to be used for short periods of time

Appliances not meant for domestic practice

Using commercial or industrial intended consumers on a domestic power supply

C. B. Hotnoga TMIET AEE BESA

A complete Guide to maximum energy savings in a domestic household

2. Gas supply to your property

Smart gas meters

Application on gas heating and hot water systems

How the make the most out of controlling your gas usage

Situations where a smart gas controller can help

When and how not to use a gas smart meter

Be your own gas meter

Gas central heating systems

Types of gas boilers

Controlling heating in your home

Radiators and heating system around the property

Maximizing the efficiency of your heating installation

Spaces with special heating needs

C. B. Hotnoga TMIET AEE BESA

A complete Guide to maximum energy savings in a domestic household

Hot water

Controlling the amount of hot water used

Hot water storage tank

Controlling when your hot water is needed

Tap and sink hot water needs

Bathing requirements

Where hot water is being wasted

Gas cooker, hob and oven

Making sure your kitchen appliances are not wasting gas

Using a gas cooker to its full potential

Hob and oven, how not to operate

Try not to do in your kitchen

3. Insulating your home

Is your home energy efficient?

Is correct insulation making a difference?

Keeping your property warm in the winter and cool in the summer without spending a fortune

Just make the most out of what you already have in place

C. B. Hotnoga TMIET AEE BESA

A complete Guide to maximum energy savings in a domestic household

4. Water supply to your property

Cold drinking water

Water supply and your provider

Maintenance charges

Where water is lost

How much water goes through your kitchen sink

Home appliances that use cold water

Washing machine

Dishwasher

Water dispensing units

Special taps

Cold bathing and washing water

Bath water

Showering

Toilet sinks

Flushing toilets

C. B. Hotnoga TMIET AEE BESA

A complete Guide to maximum energy savings in a domestic household

Hot water

Water used in your heating system

Bathing hot water

Showering

Hot water and kitchen sink

Hot water and toilet sinks

Water used in large amounts

Gardening / watering

Washing vehicles and cleaning jobs

Pools

Hot tubs and outdoor showers

C. B. Hotnoga TMIET AEE BESA

A complete Guide to maximum energy savings in a domestic household

Foreword

In my day to day work as an energy engineer, in all my years of various specialized training, practice on small, medium, large or huge energy projects, experience in countless real life challenges, being part of many institutions, associations, specialist groups, guilds or forums and dealing directly with energy experts from all possible backgrounds, conversations have always concluded and common ground was reached as: **energy is the future.**

The way we produce, harness, store and use energy is of greatest importance to all of us, and by all of us I mean not just humankind, humans as a species but, every living organism on this Blue Planet and the Planet itself. Energy keeps our homes warm, comfortable and connected to the outside world, our high streets crowded with business, hospitals, schools, transport... all essential and non essential services going. On a non-domestic scale we can think of ships sailing the seas and oceans of the world, airplanes streaming the skies, lorries moving goods and products dearly required in our day to day lives. Everything craves and uses energy. But unearthing, harnessing or producing energy comes at a heavy price for the Planet and subsequently all living organisms, including us - humans - the ones in need for energy. A vicious circle.

Petrol, natural gases, coals and other related fossil fuels we take out of the ground to then turn into energy, can only be used once and when gone they're gone (non-renewable resources). Buried treasure that took millions of years to form up makes its way to the surface with a vengeance, as burning fossil fuels releases CO_2 (carbon dioxide - a greenhouse gas) into the atmosphere and contributes to global warming.

Non-fossil sources, mainly revolving around producing electricity: nuclear, hydroelectric, solar, geothermal, wind, ... only cover a fraction of nowadays global demand for energy. These are classified as renewable resources but do cause some, or a lot, of pollution to the environment. A vicious circle indeed.

As far we know that modern human society is depending on energy and will be even more so in the future. Non-renewable resources are getting close to depletion and sustainable ones are not yet sufficient to cover the needs of keeping

11

C. B. Hotnoga TMIET AEE BESA

A complete Guide to maximum energy savings in a domestic household

the world running as we know it. Solution? Only one and not very easy: **Change**. Changing the way we all treat energy and how we use it. Engineering development and new technologies are already delivering more positive answers for the future. Better, cleaner, renewable ways of producing energy. Scientists, inventors, engineers and developers are doing their part in finding the best way forward but, we all have to make a difference in the way we see and use energy.

All people of the world, in our homes, places of work, transportation we use, anywhere we go and everything we do, each and all, we can make all the difference towards the future we want to pass on to our children. We cannot just rely or leave it to someone else. Politicians, governments, corporations, businesses big or small, are now understanding the threat presented by global warming and climate change. It doesn't matter what your financial situation is, if you are wealthy or poor, energy should not be taken for granted, even if you can afford all the energy in the world. Why? Because energy always takes its toll on the environment. Even the cleanest ways of producing, harnessing, storing or distributing energy will still cause some pollution, leave a carbon footprint. Just because you can afford it doesn't mean you should take it as a given and **waste** it.

Who can benefit from this Guide?

Everyone and anyone with a real interest in making a difference towards controlling and reducing how much energy is being used by their domestic environment. You can have, maintain or improve your lifestyle whilst cutting down on how much your property needs to supply from your electricity, gas and water providers. End result will be shown on your bills, minimum savings of at least 25% are possible to vast majority of households. How? By getting used to new habits, smarter habits and just a little bit of better judgement. Saving on electricity, gas or water doesn't mean you will have to keep your lights off, watch less television, not to use the cooker or not have a bath when you want to. Nothing like that! We are just too used not to think about it or never think about it, to let all appliances, machines, electrics and electronics in our house run in whatever way they have been built to run.

C. B. Hotnoga TMIET AEE BESA

A complete Guide to maximum energy savings in a domestic household

One little example: you have quite a smart home - and this day and age due to new technologies many people do - with LED lighting, clever central heating also controlled by a smart meter and yourself from a mobile device, energy efficient appliances throughout the property. At some point during winter you feel a little too cold in one of the bedrooms, compared to the rest of the house, and decide to improve the situation by installing an electric radiator/heater or electric heating fan rated let's say at 3kWh - most are, especially the cheaper ones. You then use this radiator a few hours a day for the next 4 months. 3 kWh means 3 kilo-Watt-hour = 3000 Watt/hour. Wattage gives rating/efficiency/how much electricity that consumer unit uses per hour, so 3000 Watt per hour. For every hour in operation this heater consumes as much as/the equivalent of:

22 TVs running at the same time, or

15 fridge-freezers, or

6 washing machines, or

30 of the old bright 100 Watt incandescent/filament light bulbs, or

about 150 of the new 10-30 Watt LED bulbs.

So, this heater will use, every hour, the equivalent of around 150 LED bulbs, all running at the same time. 1 electric heater = 150 LED lights? This can't be good business. And it is not, your meter readings for electricity will without fail register this and your provider will put it on your bill. A very expensive way of keeping one room a little warmer, one little example of not knowing how much something you plug into a socket can actually consume. And a lot of people make such mistakes by not understanding how electricity works, not understanding the energy efficiency ratings on appliances, not knowing what and how to check or just not caring.

This guide is intended to help and educate any reader, no matter the part of the world you might be living. How many or how few - more energy efficient or not - electrical appliances you have in your house, how old your property is or more cheap/expensive price on electricity/gas/water in your country, makes no

13

C. B. Hotnoga TMIET AEE BESA

A complete Guide to maximum energy savings in a domestic household

difference. In fact, older properties, dated installations, structures and designs, tend to be less energy efficient and even bigger savings can be applied to these. Think about your monthly and annual bills and if you set your mind to paying at least a quarter less, every month of every year, this guide will show you how. Not to mention helping the environment.

Introduction to energy savings

We live in a world hell-bent on consuming, we are all consumers and so the main target for anyone with something to sell. Any domestic product that runs on electricity - plugged into a socket, battery operated or hardwired to a supply point - will come with clear information/papers stating its functional energy needs, also known as classification or efficiency rating. It is the law - standards are many across the world - some countries, group of countries or unions have their own well-established standards to grade and rank every device that needs plugging or charging in order to operate. This is needed for us, the consumers, to know exactly the quality and the efficiency of that product when deciding to purchase or not.

Growing demand for a certain electrical device or type of product will then give manufacturers the incentive to come up with better quality and better efficiency. Competition between brands was and always will be beneficial to consumers as they/we will be getting better quality for money. Being aware of what you are bringing into your home and making the right decisions on how that appliance will be used, or if it is needed in the first place, will help towards reducing your energy bills.

But making savings starts with what you already have in your home, no one can ever advise you to replace everything you own with brand new, better stuff, just for the sake of being a little greener. That is crazy. We will get to the chapter advising you how to make better judgement on new appliances, when replacing something is truly needed. We start by looking at what is running in your house at this very moment and how to keep them under control. Every electrical device is built/manufactured to operate/function within certain parameters with certain energy requirements: there is very little we can do about that. What we can control

C. B. Hotnoga TMIET AEE BESA

A complete Guide to maximum energy savings in a domestic household

is the run time of these devices and where controls or adjustments are possible, to then "calibrate" our property to optimal standards.

Global warming and climate change

The threat to all life on Earth is real. The threat to, in a few generations time, not have a habitable Planet for humans is very real. We want and demand too much, consume more than we need and on top of it all: waste, waste and waste some more. From a personal perspective but based on mainly commercial and industrial energy saving projects, **waste** is what I discover **everywhere**. And a worldwide population of almost 8 billion people is just the cherry on top of the cake.

If we can so easily rely just on governments leaders, authorities and big organisations to take care of things at the larger scale, what about our own backyard? But then again, the world is run by supply and demand politics so many businesses are just giving the population what they are asking for. And this is exactly how we are now facing deplorable levels of plastics contamination, un-breathable air in and around large cities, decimated green spaces, poisoned soil and water supplies.

A change in climate, around the Globe, is accelerating its own consequences but also intensifies all other negative factors. What's bad gets worse really fast and the good, still remaining areas, cannot keep up or improve, mainly deteriorating. We can imagine, as most religions have these as concepts, a fight between Good and Evil, where Evil has gained ground really fast, Good cannot keep Evil in check and Evil is now superior in every aspect, preparing to win the last and final battle.

Us humans, we've always had a craving towards finding that common and supreme enemy, a deadly threat to all of us: young, old, rich, poor. No matter who or where you are, that enemy is here: **fast global warming and accelerated climate change.**

C. B. Hotnoga TMIET AEE BESA

A complete Guide to maximum energy savings in a domestic household

Purpose of guide Provide real life examples and practical steps	**Gather** **Test** **Monitor** **Share**	Energy saving ideas Workable solutions Best practices Feasible and productive approaches
Energy savings Electricity, gas + water	**Constant** **Measurable** **Continuous**	Significant Controllable Considerable
Plan of action	**ASSESSMENT** **PLANNING** **IMPLEMENTATION** **ADJUSTMENT** **MONITORING**	Improve efficiency Raise awareness Change perceptions Minimise effect of bad habits Worldwide sharing platform
Target	**Existing** Buildings and structures Conditions and systems Designs and outlays	Making the most out of what we already have to work with. Recommend better alternatives, more energy efficient approaches and behaviours.
How	**Make adjustments** **Calibrate irregularities** **Rectify failures** **Change parameters** **Set up run times**	Improve: Efficiency Functionality Reliability Needs
Home specific features **and requirements**	**Knowledge of your own** **home and what runs inside** **of it**	Recommended Feasible and workable No disruption
Practice	End of month meter readings: **Electricity** **Gas** **Water**	Periodic monitoring. Comparison to same month of previous year, seasonal, 6 monthly and annual. Patience and observation.
Results	**Analyse and demonstrate to** **yourself**	Get used to new habits Know what is going on Be in control

16

C. B. Hotnoga TMIET AEE BESA

A complete Guide to maximum energy savings in a domestic household

1. Electricity

Smart meters

Applications for electric consumers

Smart meters, exactly as specified in their name, are designed and made to meter/measure the amount of energy used at place of installation, normally placed inside or vicinity of mains electrical intake to your property, will send a wireless signal to a monitoring device inside your home. So an electric smart meter will normally come as a 2 part install: measuring unit(must be installed by a qualified electrician) and information/monitoring screen(that tells us how much electricity is being used by our household at time being and also registering daily, weekly, monthly... totals).

Main function is given by wireless method of having our electric readings right in front of our eyes, without the need of going to physically check at place of installation. They will also be capable of sending these accurate readings directly to your energy supplier, so will save you the job, and through use of an App give you remote access from mobile devices: smartphone, tablet, computer.

A brief mention: my property in the UK was equipped by energy supplier with an electricity and gas smart metering system, two separate installations that are sending readings to same monitoring device showing me both gas and electric. Smart meters themselves must always be installed by qualified electrician and gas safe engineer respectively. Because not all over the world consumers will have both gas and electric under same system, or no smart metering at all, I have put these under different sections of this Guide: electric and then gas.

C. B. Hotnoga TMIET AEE BESA

A complete Guide to maximum energy savings in a domestic household

How to put an electric smart meter to good use

I meet a lot of people still thinking that installing a smart meter will give you energy savings right from the start. That is not the case. At the very least it will make you more conscious of what is going on in your house and then, month by month offer better visibility by comparison. A smart meter will save you the trouble of sending monthly or quarterly readings to your supplier and also having to access, crawl or tumble to find and access the meter itself.

More advanced smart metering systems will give remote control of your home heating system and thermostat, allowing to turn the heating up from your mobile device before getting home. We are not talking here of smart homes or homes of the future, this Guide is intended to help the general public and show were savings can be made on existing designs and systems, the way your home is now.

The BIG secret when saving on energy is to compare how much you've used in the month just gone with the same month of previous year. Example: Let's say it is now February and you have readings on how much electricity was used throughout the month of January. Compare January of this year with January of previous year. This will give you proof on what you have saved and that confidence of doing the right thing. Only by comparing same month of different years will give an accurate idea, due to many parts of the world January(example) being a winter month, or the other way around if on the other side of the Globe. Seasons, weather and outdoor temperatures (very cold or too hot) have greatest impact on how much energy we use. Followed by adding or removing big consumers to our property (pool, hot tub, air conditioning) and changing energy supplier or/and change in energy price. This is why we compare how much energy we've used and not the price we've paid.

C. B. Hotnoga TMIET AEE BESA

A complete Guide to maximum energy savings in a domestic household

Where a smart meter can help

Smart electrical meters will help you stay more in control of your property and everything running inside of it. Once in your habit to every now and again check that average household demand for electricity and being aware where the numbers should be, it is then very easy to spot big variations. A perfect tool to alert you when something goes over the limit, how much running that air conditioning is going to cost you, installing Christmas lights, fitting a hot tub or just for comparison purposes, how much energy your household is using – before and after - all examples of big consumers that will input a considerable amount on power demand, but also a good device to tell us when something we've changed or adjusted is delivering that desired result.

Yes, we can use the smart meter as "in front of our eyes and real time" proof towards doing something right, or wrong. If your property is quite large and you have a lot of big consumers running at the same time, a newly installed smart meter will tell you how much energy one device is using – check the readings before and after switching than unit on. All households will have pre-installed appliances that we are totally unsure how much energy they're using; it is interesting to check that against meter readings and then put in balance if that consumer is actually needed to run, maybe run it for shorter periods of time or adjust settings(if any) to make it more energy efficient.

Where a smart meter cannot help

A smart meter will help us monitor "real time" demands for electrical energy around the house. But we are still the ones to identify which consumer is using what and make judgement on maybe using that appliance less, adjust its run time or re-calibrate functions: temperature and run time of air conditioning, water heaters or coolers, washing machine, fridge-freezer, electric space heaters or coolers and list can continue for most bigger units.

A list of "worst offenders" – big consumers of electricity in your home – will include:

- Space/habitat temperature control: heating, air conditioning

C. B. Hotnoga TMIET AEE BESA

A complete Guide to maximum energy savings in a domestic household

- Recreational environments: pool, hot tub
- Charging of electrical vehicle
- Non-domestic activities: garage work (welding, use of power tools), steam washers, use of hired equipment
- Garden work with use of heavy-duty equipment
- Water heaters or coolers
- Washing machine and dryer
- Dishwasher
- Ventilation and extractor fans
- Fridge and/or freezer
- Other kitchen appliances
- Entertainment: Television, TV boxes and home cinema, Internet
- Lighting
- Home security

Be your own "electric smart meter"

Please take note on difference between smart meter and smart thermostat. A smart home heating/temperature control thermostat will mainly help keep habitational parameters where desired, maybe save some little money – a mix between gas central heating and electrical controls. A smart meter will help keep under radar everything using energy around the property and can be both electricity and gas. With so much going on in our day to day lives it is very easy to lose track on which consumers are "draining our pot" and causing that energy bill to skyrocket.

Be wiser on what you are bringing into your home. If not used to checking energy efficiency ratings on electrical goods, or never done it before, just ask the seller to explain it to you, show you where on the appliance or instruction manual to find it. Energy ratings are many and different standards across the world, but any new product will have clear mention on this. Higher efficiency - less energy used - pay less on bills.

To identify which of your existing electricals are big consumers of energy, check the product for stickers or labels. Examples:

C. B. Hotnoga TMIET AEE BESA

A complete Guide to maximum energy savings in a domestic household

- A domestic fridge average power consumption is typically between 100 and 250 watts, depending on size, performance and a few other factors. This translates as 100 to 250 watt per hour. So over a full day this fridge is likely to use between 1 to 2.5 kilowatt/hours (kWh). A very rough estimate will put annual running cost between 100(pound, dollar, euro) and 250(pound, dollar, euro) per fridge.
- A domestic dishwasher average power consumption is typically between 1200 and 2400 watts every hour or 1.2 to 2.4 kWh. If we are to use this dishwasher for 10 hours a day, same as the fridge (fridge will run for approximately 10 hours daily due to "taking a break" once temperature is reached) would mean a power consumption between 12 to 24 kWh daily. Rough annual estimate based across averages will put electrical running cost between 1,200(pound, dollar, euro) and 2,400(pound, dollar, euro) per dishwasher.

Can totally appreciate that no one on this Planet (unless doing dishwashing for the whole neighbourhood) will be using a dishwasher for 10 hours a day, but for educational purposes only, the message is clear – a dishwasher is about 10 times more expensive to run compared to a fridge. So a more serious/big consumer that we can try to use only when needed, once fully loaded to avoid unnecessary run times and save on electricity AND water.

So check the label/sticker/compliance plate or manual for wattage (electrical energy this appliance will be consuming for every hour in use.) Always be more mindful when values are shown as kW rather that W because 1kW(kilowatt) = 1000W(watt) a good indication this consumer is expensive to have in running condition.

Lighting your property

Indoor lighting

LED(light-emitting diode) luminaires and light bulbs have been around for some good few years. They have been continuously improved, life span increased to

C. B. Hotnoga TMIET AEE BESA

A complete Guide to maximum energy savings in a domestic household

tens of thousands of hours on most types. LED light fittings and bulbs/tubes are electronic devices that will give off light when receiving an electrical current(power). Majority of electronic devices (compared to electric) will run on a low current and that makes them a lot more energy efficient and using very low amounts of energy.

Power input on LED lighting is still amounted in W(watts) but their brightness is measured in Lumens - total amount of visible light generated -. For your information, LED lighting comes in 3 main shades of white to choose from – or colour temperatures: warm white, cool white and daylight.

Examples:

A 10W LED bulb is the equivalent of a 60W standard incandescent light bulb, giving a brightness of 700+ lumens.

An 18W LED bulb is the equivalent of a 100W standard incandescent light, giving a brightness of 1300+ lumens.

This will vary slightly depending on manufacturer and price range, but one thing is for certain: LED lighting is a lot cheaper to run than conventional standard incandescent bulbs. Also cheaper than all other previous types: halogen or CFL (compact fluorescent light - also called energy saving bulbs before the launch of LED).

Upgrading your lighting to LED is definitely something to take into consideration. LED bulbs will pretty much earn their value back in energy saved and also have a much longer life span. Start by changing one or a few at a time, when new light bulbs are needed.

External lighting

Most common type of external lighting are floodlights, also known as security lights, normally very bright and spreading light over larger areas. For other categories of external light fittings – wall lights or lamp posts that have replaceable bulbs – please see above option of upgrading light bulbs with LED, especially if

C. B. Hotnoga TMIET AEE BESA

A complete Guide to maximum energy savings in a domestic household

running throughout the night. Always make sure a light fitting is rated and safe for external use: waterproof, fit for purpose.

Floodlights have historically been known to use a lot of energy: halogen and high-pressure sodium lamps. This until the appearance of LED fittings, much cheaper to run and greater longevity. LED floodlights are manufactured as single integral unit, no bulb or tube to replace so when something goes wrong there is no other option but to replace the whole thing. With this in mind, they are still the best option.

PIR(passive infrared) sensors, also known as motion detection sensors are another improvement to consider for external lighting that is needed for security purposes, to only activate when something or someone is moving in front of sensor. This will save energy.

Types of light fittings and bulbs

Light bulbs:

- Incandescent – traditional but not energy efficient, many parts of the world have stopped production.
- LED – Light Emitting Diode, currently the most energy efficient from all types .
- HID – High Intensity Discharge, mainly for commercial and industrial use to create as much visible light as possible: warehouses, street lights, large spaces.
- Compact Fluorescent (CFL) – give a more comfortable to eyes light, closest to LED as efficiency.
- Linear Fluorescent – long tubes or strips, are energy efficient and can also be found as LED.
- Speciality – a type of lighting that is becoming more and more popular, mainly for decorative purposes due to multiple colours given ambiance, made only from environment-friendly materials.

Light fittings:

C. B. Hotnoga TMIET AEE BESA

A complete Guide to maximum energy savings in a domestic household

This section is intended to describe application of luminaires for their purpose and feasible location/point of installation and use. Most common shapes of lamp holders/cap or base of a light bulb are: Bayonet cap, Edison screw cap, Capsule lamps, Linear, Spotlights, long Tubes.

Ceiling lights have most practical indoor application. Depending on your necessities and comfort, also take energy efficiency into consideration.

Wall mounted light. Whatever the purpose, better alternatives can always be found, even if just replacing the bulb with LED equivalent.

Table lights: reading, study, bedside or decorative – make sure they are not costing you more than they should.

External, garage, bollard, ground lights – we now have the LED option on everything.

Special occasion lighting, Security, Christmas/Holidays lights, etc.

Throwing or organising a party on a special event might turn your property into a much bigger energy consumer than it normally is. Some people will end up hiring all sorts of commercial devices: special extremely powerful lighting, sound/speakers, photography mirrors, special effects – fog, mist, water balloons, snow machines... you name it. These devices are well known to demand a lot of power and even if intended to be used for short periods, there always is a lot more you can do to control run time and better efficiency. First of all make sure you fully understand how these work under optimal conditions, then only keep running when truly needed.

Christmas lighting and electrically powered decorations are loved in many countries. Old types of festive lights and illuminations used to double or even triple electricity bills for the month of December. Nowadays LED devices have opened the door to never ending possibilities, unfortunately still pollutant and not friendly to the environment but using less energy. Keep in control by reducing running time from entire night to few hours every evening.

24

C. B. Hotnoga TMIET AEE BESA

A complete Guide to maximum energy savings in a domestic household

Security lighting, as also described in section above, works best as LED fixtures with PIR (motion detection) or daylight photocell sensor that will switch on the light depending on setting: when there is movement in front of light or at night fall, to then run for a period of time adjusted on timer.

Live smart not to live in the dark

Lighting is essential in our households, improving our livelihoods. We cannot do or go without. Options are countless, applications without restriction and only limited by imagination. With better understanding and just a small amount of better judgement we can make not just significant but considerable savings.

"Switch it off and you will make all the difference!" is still a relevant motto. If not using that space, room or area it makes sense to switch all lights off behind you. Also upgrade to LED when and where possible, start with all light bulbs around the house. Use of timers and motion detection sensors is also advised. Pay more attention to bigger consumers.

Ring circuits/Sockets and device charging points

Mobile devices charge points

With so much technology surrounding us these days and most households using multiple mobile devices: smartphones, tablets, laptops, various gaming consoles... and so much more, it is very easy to lose track on how much charging and keeping these devices running might cost you. General thinking is "charging mobile devices is using little energy so it won't be expensive". Not far from the truth, putting a device on charge for a couple of hours won't cost you the world. But the next question becomes, how many devices are you putting on charge on a daily basis, 5 – 10 – 15? And maybe more than once a day. Not to mention nowadays we also have to charge: cordless vacuum cleaners, battery powered tools, battery chargers for re-charging batteries, electronic cigarettes, torches and other lights, children's electric toys, electric toothbrush, other beauty and cosmetic related items, etc. Believe everyone got the gist by now, the list of items we will eventually need to put on charge is huge.

25

C. B. Hotnoga TMIET AEE BESA

A complete Guide to maximum energy savings in a domestic household

When we need something to be charged we'll have to put it on charge, it is not a matter of doing it but how and for how long. Beware of so called chargers – for everything really, they come in so many shapes and functions – also known as adapters and/or transformers because they will "adapt" or "transform" the energy/power coming from a socket into what that device needs to charge as and then function. Majority of these chargers / transformers / adapters will still continue to use some electricity after the device was fully charged and even after the device was removed/unplugged from charger, as long as still connected to the power supply/socket. Not as much energy as when charging, a lot less but depending on how many you have around the house and how often they're being used, with time they will make a difference.

In the UK we use so called "switched" socket outlets and other power supply points: spurs, extension leads. So when we want to stop that socket from using any power or make sure no power is coming out of that socket we have the option of switching it off, just like a light switch on the front of the socket outlet itself. Will give exactly the same result as unplugging everything from that socket/extension lead but without the "unplugging" part. A very clever and handy option as we can always make sure nothing is coming out of that power supply. Example: If we have 1 extension lead connected to a socket and 5 different devices plugged/supplied from that extension lead, by switching the socket on the wall off, all of the devices would power down and we are 100% certain all energy use from that power outlet has stopped.

When charging or running any sort of a device from charger, best practice would be that when device is fully charged to unplug it from charger and also unplug charger from socket outlet, or switch the socket off if you have the option. Some energy will still be used when device is fully charged but still on charge. Some energy will still be used by charger itself still being plugged to socket, even if no device is present. Especially when leaving home for longer periods of time, make sure everything you don't need/want to still consume energy is disconnected from power outlet. Unplug all from socket.

TVs, computers and other screens

C. B. Hotnoga TMIET AEE BESA

A complete Guide to maximum energy savings in a domestic household

Main intention behind putting these household devices under the same section is to demonstrate that: television sets, TV boxes, computers, gaming consoles(Xbox, PlayStation, other), home cinema, smart speakers, Internet hubs, other smart devices – will still use energy after being Switched OFF from power button or remote control OFF button (not the same thing as powered down or removed from power supply).

None of these, taken one by one, are massive consumers of energy. We all love home entertainment and will usually have in our homes multiple outlets and versions of watching television, films/movies, Box Sets over the Internet, all sorts of gaming gadgets. The energy needed to run everything, all of these put together, is of considerable amount. A TV box will continue to download or record programs for you when TV is off. A gaming console will continue to download and upgrade itself in OFF mode. Smart speakers are always "on the listen". Main lesson to be learned here is: if not needed, make sure they are not just powered off or powered down but, unplugged from power source/socket outlet.

Fridge freezers and electric cookers

British version of what we call a fridge freezer is normally a single unit, part fridge (usually top), part freezer (bottom). Fully aware other nations would call the same household appliance a refrigerator, just fridge or just freezer and such units also come with single function of fridge /refrigeration and freezer /freezing single module. A domestic fridge freezer is nothing to be afraid of and would normally cost you, in energy used, between 100 and 200 (pounds, dollars, euros) per whole year of having it in continuous use, depending on size, functions and other features. Freezers tend to be more expensive to run than fridges due to having to keep much lower temperatures. Make sure settings and temperatures are correct, cheapest option is to have such appliances at desired temperatures and every now and then defrost, for cleaning and manufacturer guidance/recommended maintenance. They will consume more energy when often powered down/defrosted and then to reach set temperatures.

C. B. Hotnoga TMIET AEE BESA

A complete Guide to maximum energy savings in a domestic household

Electric cookers, on the other hand, are big consumers of electricity. Definitely much more expensive to run than gas hob and/or oven. If you do not have the option for gas, or no gas in your area, then having the right sort of an appliance can save or waste you a significant amount of money (annual basis). Put together as electric cookers or single hob or oven, these units will use starting from 3 kw/hour and as high as 8 kW/hour, which is more than double. A good brand/manufacturer will save you money, even if a little more expensive to buy from new, in the long run you will see the difference. Always check the energy efficiency rating. A quick search on the Internet will give you a lot of options, client satisfaction after a long time in use will guide you in making the right choice. Once your electric hub/oven is at desired temperature, keep it there until cooking is finished, allowing to cool off and then heat back up again will use a lot of electricity. Keep running only as long as needed. If and when at point of purchasing a new one, remember that some makes will cost you "an arm and a leg" to run, even if just for a few hours a week, difference on energy efficiency between manufacturers can be huge.

Washing machines and tumble dryers

Washers and dryers are another extremely competent example of how important energy performance standards can be. Washing machines can use between 400 to 1300 Watts per hour, so you can easily end up with one that will cost you 3 times more energy than it should. To make things even more interesting, a tumble dryer will use roughly 3 times more energy than a washing machine. None of this is rocket science. White goods – large electrical goods used domestically – are known to be manufactured by many different companies, under different prices - normally explained in quality, reliability, life span and energy efficiency.

A washing machine of a good brand/name might cost you a bit more when purchasing but it will earn its money back by lasting longer, saving you on electricity and doing a better job. You can always search wholesaler prices for discounts, offers or bargains, maybe end up buying that better-quality appliance cheaper than a lesser equivalent from a different manufacturer. Tumble dryers must heat up, normally anything that produces heat is expensive on energy. If you can manage without one - all the better - if not, make sure to only use it for short

C. B. Hotnoga TMIET AEE BESA

A complete Guide to maximum energy savings in a domestic household

periods of time. When looking for that brand new one, do not buy a poor rated model.

Dishwashers and other high energy consumers

Long have dishwashers been the subject of pro and against arguments. Due to using considerable amounts of energy and also water. As specified from the very beginning, this Guide is not intended to convince you on not using home appliances, or buying new stuff, that would mean spending money – not saving; only to advise on better judgement. The idea is for you to enjoy energy savings (accompanied by financial savings) as result of better using everything present in your household at time being. If it comes to replacing, buying new appliances, strongest advice goes towards highly rated energy efficient goods.

Any machine with functions on heating air or water, will tend to use high amounts of energy. Electric cooker is worst offender followed by tumble dryer, dishwasher, washing machine. And we've not yet mentioned: deep oil fryer, water heater (kettle), microwave/oven, toaster, sandwich makers, food preparing/processing/mixing/cooking/steaming/boiling kitchen robots. The list can go on a very long while and it really makes you think how many kitchen appliances we end up using in our homes, most of the times giving no thought to how pricey they are to run. Giving no thought to how energy efficient they were before buying, in the first place.

What you don't really want is to end up running a big consumer for a long time, with a potential for that unit in one go to be using more energy than all of your lighting throughout the household, or more energy than all TVs, computers, entertainment – put together. And some white goods do have this potential. We live in a modern, prosperous world and want to have it all. Nothing wrong with that. But there is still so much stuff surrounding us, or already in our homes, so many appliances that make very little sense to even have them in use; will be consuming a lot of expensive energy towards a very little, if not insignificant result. Be in the know, any machine rated to use more than 200 Watt per hour should make you wonder how long you need it in use for. Anything using more than 1 kW/hour should make you think if you really want to use it or can get the same result a

C. B. Hotnoga TMIET AEE BESA

A complete Guide to maximum energy savings in a domestic household

different way. And if you do plug it in, make sure it is for limited amounts of time, only when truly required.

Cold/Hot water dispensing units

These are more and more popular for family use, same as a water boiler or water dispensing cooler at your place of work: offices, canteens, staff rooms, receptions, waiting rooms. Unfortunately, these machines are still running with commercial energy demands rather than domestic and main characteristic is having to be connected to a source of energy continuously, so you can have cold or hot drinking water at any time. Something like this will generously add to your energy bill. There are fridges with function of dispensing cold water and the British favourite way of heating up water is use of a kettle. Kettle being a considerable consumer of electricity on its own.

Always mindful of what you plug into a socket

We've tried to mention most "culprits", consumers that might secretly take our energy bill to new highs. As a list it can continue beyond imagination itself. New inventions, technology, products, appliances are coming out every day. Demand and supply. We like something so we'll be asking for it. Manufacturers will make sure to sell that something to us. Good or not so good? Wisdom is key. Why spend on something you don't really need in the first place. Then why spend on something that is not performing well, not reliable, not efficient, not delivering a good result for value? Have a look around you. Pretty sure you can identify a few of these unnecessarily big consumers around you at this very moment in time. It only takes a few seconds to find that sticker or plate on the appliance with performance rating and energy demand(wattage). And if you realise that one appliance is 5 or 10 times more expensive for every hour in use compared to your washing machine or fridge, or TV? Do you still want to plug it into a socket? How long for? Make the right call. This is how energy savings take shape: reducing, adjusting, knowing what is what.

30

C. B. Hotnoga TMIET AEE BESA

A complete Guide to maximum energy savings in a domestic household

Big consumer units with special requirements or protection

Hot tubs and other leisure domestic outlets

General public view is that only wealthy people can afford a hot tub at home. Not so much these days when inflatable, portable and easy to install bubble baths can be purchased for affordable digits. We will not go into a totally specialised area represented by: domestic pools, steam rooms, sauna rooms, high capacity hot tubs – keeping our feet on the ground – energy demands for such "ventures" are indeed huge, compared to average domestic household. Price of heating up and keeping large amounts of water at desired temperature + warming up the space + filtration +++ will come to a total much higher than energy consumption for whole average property without such amenities. Even on such occasions, more energy efficient installations will have a great impact on bills.

Going back to more common domestic leisure hot tubs, once water is at desired temperature, keep the unit running to maintain that temperature. Allowing a large body of water to cool down and then reheat is more expensive than keeping set temperature once achieved. Hot tubs will come with covers and other means of protection against loss of temperature when not in use. If planning to use a hot tub for a number of days, make sure it is well insulated (cover tightly on), safe for bathers (water quality – treated with hot-tub chemicals) and use that water for as long as practical, before emptying to refresh. A lot cheaper to run if located indoors with other means of space heating, water temperature won't be quickly lost. If your only option is to have one outdoors, summertime operation will be a lot cheaper than winter.

Garden electrical tools

Another new "trend" is for people to hire/rent different types of equipment, rather than buying or owning a machine/home appliance, and then self-deliver on all sorts of domestic jobs: steam cleaning, jet washing, carpet/rug cleaning, mixing building materials, running power tools... so much more. And when it makes total sense, saving you money to do it yourself rather than paying someone

C. B. Hotnoga TMIET AEE BESA

A complete Guide to maximum energy savings in a domestic household

else for the works, where builders or paid handymen will still be using hired tools supplied from your mains; please do not forget that most of these machines are built and intended for commercial use. They will work in a domestic environment but tend to use a lot of energy.

Garage and workshop electrical units

Many of us will have a domestic working environment: office, workshop, garage, garden shed, separate room in the house... It all depends on everyone's personal and specific circumstances: DIY jobs, hobbies, interests, also on the rise – part-time or full-time work from home – running a small business from home/small manufacturing/crafting/repairs, etc. Activities will vary and use of electrically powered devices is common.

From use of small power tools to welding and even running industrial machinery, provided that electrical installation can cope with demand, people will try and do it all. Some consumers might be small, not really putting your energy bills under strain; others – have the potential to exponentially increase it. You are the only one to know. Be aware of energy requirements, add this cost to your other needs and put in balance if worth the trouble or not. Heavy machinery, certain types of equipment, power tools or plant; are built and intended for industrial and commercial use for some very good reasons: safety, compliance, control, feasibility, efficiency. Good judgement on everything mentioned here will make a huge difference to your energy bills.

Electrical vehicle charging points

Future of automotive industry is electric. It is now written in UK law that manufacturing and sale of new automobiles running on fossil fuels (diesel and petrol) will be banned from year 2040, possibly as early as 2032, to reach effectively zero carbon emissions. The whole European Union and many other countries around the world have similar plans, dates and targets will slightly vary. Natural resources of oil are soon to be depleted, levels of pollution at an all-time high, global warming and melting of glaciers/ice caps accelerated to unprecedented levels, sea levels rising with other consequences of climate change already affecting hundreds of millions of people. Our only hope towards preserving as much of the existing Planet

C. B. Hotnoga TMIET AEE BESA

A complete Guide to maximum energy savings in a domestic household

as we know it is change. Change in how we see time present and the future, change in needs and behaviours.

If you already own a fully electrical vehicle then you need to charge it from home. Technology is continuously advancing and improving, charging points are faster, better, more efficient. You do not have to stay faithful to same make of a charging station as the vehicle, if one was supplied with vehicle. There are many options on so called "universal" home charging points and manufacturers are fighting each other in coming out with better performing units. Same as any electrical outlets, energy efficiency makes all the difference. Check rating before buying. Remember to unplug your vehicle from charger when battery/batteries are full and also switch off/power down charging unit as it will still continue to use some energy, even if no load is present.

Electrical outlets/Big consumer units to avoid

Electric radiators, heating fans

Any form of heating that will use electricity as source of energy is a bad idea. Unless you have no other choices, maybe under special circumstances or events, to be used for limited periods of time only but not as definitive solution or continuous use. Electric radiators will start from about 1 kWh and go up to 3 kWh. Electric fan heaters power consumption will be higher, from about 2 kWh to 5 kWh and above. An expensive way to keep a room/space/area warm.

Old/dated appliances

This day and age where technological development is reaching never before even imagined grounds, where same type of a domestic hardware looks entirely different from how it used to 10 or 20 years ago; people will be holding on to appliances and devices that have passed the test of time, still trustworthy and

C. B. Hotnoga TMIET AEE BESA

A complete Guide to maximum energy savings in a domestic household

doing the job. That is totally to be appreciated, we can talk about energy savings and efficiency ratings, one main polluting factor remains household devices that are replaced by owners too early and when not truly needed. Makers are competing with each other in frequently launching new products, more desirable, more attractive to consumers, maybe little more energy efficient. Well known that quality and lifespan is not what it used to be and appliances are now built to last a while but when something goes wrong cannot be mended or repair is more expensive than buying brand new. Another vicious circle.

We are split between holding on to old stuff that is still reliable but not so energy efficient - using more electricity to run – and getting rid of something dated to in return purchase a newer version that is less enduring. Unwritten laws on RECYCLING, if can be called so, will not really give optimal results. We are too hasty with "impulse buys" because we can, we can afford to or following trends – doing what everybody else does – newly released "trendy" devices are very attractive. Think for yourself, this Guide is about energy savings and saving you money as direct result of saving energy, cannot advise on what should or should not have your fancy. REDUCE energy consumption – REUSE appliances that are still in good working condition but not costing you a fortune to run – RECYCLE what is no longer optimal or feasible but make informed decisions on new replacements; this is the slogan for Recycling but also works very well in conjunction with energy savings.

Machines and units not fit for purpose

How many times have you realised something you was attempting or struggling with achieving at home was futile due to not doing it right or using the wrong appliance/machine/device? It happens to all of us, DIY-ing or desperate to get something done with whatever we have at hand. We will all keep the odd: power drill, electric heater for winter, cooling fan for summer, jet wash, carpet cleaner, corded lawn mower... you name it – stored and forgotten somewhere, just in case we might need to use it at some point. If these consumers are still in good working condition and won't end up tripping our electrical installation, wisely used for limited periods of time, all is good.

We can cook 1 chip/1 French fry in 15 litres of cooking oil in a deep fryer, can try to clean a Television set by jet washing it or check if that industrial 3D Printer

C. B. Hotnoga TMIET AEE BESA

A complete Guide to maximum energy savings in a domestic household

purchased very cheaply from a car boot sale will work when powered from our house electrical mains. Some actions can be very costly, others ill advised. We have to think for ourselves, learn how devices operate before operating them. If there are better, wiser ways of achieving same result, should be considered. Health and Safety should always come first, a brief Risk Assessment – making sure you know what your doing and how to use the unit about to power up – has never hurt anyone but the result of rushed/uninformed actions just might.

Appliances not to be used in a domestic environment

Inventory can be without number. We have explained how many people would engage in work-from-home or "Do It Yourself" tasks, making a full or part time income by working from the comfort of their own dwelling. Use of electrically powered devices will at times be inevitable, to some extent not intended for domestic use. Industrial units will normally need a 3-phase power supply to operate, a main trait for heavy machinery. It is not uncommon for small business owners to upgrade electricity supply to their household, or have both single or 3-phase options, intended for: heavy duty power tools, small production lines, small manufacturing, hobbies, crafts, handmade items, etc.

Please make sure to stay on the right side of the Law. Certain activities are not to be performed in residential areas, equipment you are using might be working just fine as powered from domestic electrical mains but: too loud, dangerous, causing other distress to neighbours – vibration, bad smell. Examples are too many and diverse, if really keen on making energy savings but at the same time running industrial and/or commercial consumers, it might be harder to see significant and constant improvements. This is an area where only extremely calculated and objective judgement will give good results.

Consumer units that will trip or damage domestic electrical installations

Resuming from above big consumers of electricity, a different outcome might occur when attempting to power up a device not intended for domestic operation or, finding your electrical mains not able to cope with demand and tripping during use. RCD protection (Residual Current Disconnection devices) are a legal requirement in many countries and new homes will be designed and supplied

C. B. Hotnoga TMIET AEE BESA

A complete Guide to maximum energy savings in a domestic household

with such protection against electrical shock and other potentially dangerous situations. These have different names around the world, will be installed inside distribution board (fuse board) to secure a whole electrical circuit or more locally: RCD protected socket (mainly outdoor), switches (mains isolators) and extension leads.

In older homes and domestic dwellings, it is extremely likely to cause serious damage to electrical installation by plugging in (or any other way of powering up a big electric consumer, such as hardwiring) a load that is too high for circuit to hold, even worse if device is faulty. So with no protective device to almost instantly disconnect electricity flow you can find yourself in real danger, electrical shorts do not necessarily have to be caused by physical damage – cutting a live cable by mistake, plugging in a defect consumer – but also overloading the circuit that might result in: melting plugs, sockets catching fire or whole installation blowing from or inside the fuse box.

Heating up your home

Smart thermostats

We are still under the electrical section of this Guide so will explain the benefits of having a static or remotely controlled – smart thermostat – installed to a heating system supplied from electrical mains only. Electrically powered boilers are still more expensive to run compared to gas. Technology is improving so if gas supply is not an option in your area then better control over indoor space and hot water temperatures is an answer towards reducing costs. By adjusting the thermostat you can "ask your electric boiler to fire up" and heat up the house to a desired set point before getting home, set up and alter run times, desired temperature and supply of hot water for household use.

Electric heating systems

36

C. B. Hotnoga TMIET AEE BESA

A complete Guide to maximum energy savings in a domestic household

Electric central heating is becoming more and more popular, not only due to gas supply restrictions in different parts of the world but people wanting to reduce their carbon footprint. Electricity is more expensive than gas or oil but it is available in almost every populated corner of the Planet. There are a number of technologies that can be installed easily – and relatively cheaply – in a wide range of homes. If gas is available in the property or nearby, then you may want to consider fitting gas central heating instead. It will be more expensive to fit than many electric systems but will be cheaper to run. Mainly about what is more important to you. Governments in many countries will be offering a grant / payment to encourage people towards considering a form of low carbon heating that –same as gas– can be expensive to install but as a renewable system cheaper overall in the long term, as well as reducing your carbon emissions.

Electric boilers

An electric boiler uses electricity rather than gas to heat hot water. Just like a gas boiler, it will heat up the water that warms your radiators, and the water you use in the kitchen and bathroom. They can come in various shapes, energy demands and sizes but in all electric boilers water will be running through the system to be heated by a heating element – similar to the way a kettle works. Can be convenient to install and up to a point also energy efficient, but there are some drawbacks when compared to a gas boiler.

Water heaters

Will give you the option of suppling fresh, hot or boiling water instantly on demand 24 hours a day. They provide a sufficient amount of hot or boiling water suitable for drinking or the washing of hands with no storage cylinder required, direct from cold mains supply. Compared to a boiler being used to heat large amounts of water for heating the entire household – central heating systems, showers, hot taps – these heaters work as dispensers of drinking water, which can be filtered. Available in all shapes and sizes, ready for a range of possible scenarios, if truly needed in your household will give the comfort of not having to put the kettle on or heat some water up on the cooker. Unfortunately, more energy efficient brands will be visibly more expensive.

C. B. Hotnoga TMIET AEE BESA

A complete Guide to maximum energy savings in a domestic household

Shower heaters

Electric showers are heating cold water with electricity. They never run out of hot water, so a good solution if you have lots of people in the house to shower one after another. These work in much the same way as electric boilers and other water heaters by sending an electric current through a heating element that gets very hot. If you already have a central heating system (gas, electric, biomass, etc.) it is recommended to have your showers (and all other non-drinking hot water outlets for that matter) supplied from it as basically using water that was already heated up once. Where not possible, all wisdom comes from buying the right energy efficient make, even if a little more expensive to purchase, will save you money if using frequently. Energy demands will vary from 5kWh to 12kWh and above. Not being savvy in this instance can turn taking a shower into an expensive business.

Tap heaters

Another gaining in popularity kitchen "apparatus", an electric tap heater will provide instant hot water on demand with virtually no waiting time. Same principles as dispensing units for potable hot water, only attached to an existing tap or whole electric faucet on its own. Same result – of giving you instant hot water – can be achieved in many ways. We have already given plenty examples of "options", some not to install in your homes even if given to you for free. It is just not worth it, putting minimal "ease" before what will turn out costing you tens if not hundreds of dollars/euros/pounds per year is not good judgement.

Cooling your home

Air conditioning

Cooling down your home should help you get a better night's sleep and give that extra comfort during very hot summer days/nights. Air conditioning is common in commercial premises – shops, offices – indoor spaces that are normally used/accessed by a lot of people. Fixed air conditioners are also known as split-units due to having both indoor and outdoor components. The indoor unit is installed on

C. B. Hotnoga TMIET AEE BESA

A complete Guide to maximum energy savings in a domestic household

wall or above the room/space to be temperature controlled, and the outdoor unit is fixed to the wall or installed on the ground outside.

Such an install is ideal if you have a room that regularly gets very hot. It is a secure way of air conditioning your home, no need to leave windows open, also quieter and usually more efficient than standalone units. Installation can only (legally) be done by a qualified air conditioning engineer. Tend to be more expensive to purchase than movable/standalone units. For energy efficiency it is recommended to reduce use to just one room, keeping doors open or trying to cool down the whole house from just one unit will cause it to run continuously.

Portable air conditioning units

Portable/standalone air conditioners, also known as single-unit, will give you the option of supplying/powering from a mains power source/socket. A venting hose at back of the unit will need to blow the hot air outside. Not as effective but will cool your space without the need of a permanent installation. Can then be moved around/re-located from room to room by venting hot air out the window or door. Can be un-plugged and placed in storage when not in use. Can pose a security risk if left unattended, open window/door. Some models can be extremely heavy, overheat and a drip tray will need emptying due to condensation building up inside the unit; forgetting to do so will cause a leak back into the room. Not as effective at cooling as split-unit air conditioners, will mainly offer a significant drop in temperature when in use, once switched off temperatures in the area will quickly reinstate.

Fixed and mobile ventilation fans

A fan at its most basic level simply moves air, it doesn't cool the air. By creating airflow, the sweat on your skin can evaporate which lowers body temperature. Air circulators don't just move a bit of air at your face to create the illusion of cooling, they displace all the air in the entire room to actually make you feel cooler. Firstly you will need to consider which fan fits your requirements, the size of your room will determine what you choose. For a small room or office you don't need much more than a desk or tower fan - larger spaces something more powerful.

C. B. Hotnoga TMIET AEE BESA

A complete Guide to maximum energy savings in a domestic household

Efficient cooling ideas that work

Keep your blinds closed, 30 percent of unwanted heat comes from your windows. Closing the shades/curtains/blinds prevents your home from becoming a miniature greenhouse, especially the case with south and west facing windows.

Install backout curtains, will block sunlight, naturally insulating the rooms in which they're installed to reduce heat gain.

Closing off unused doors will prevent cool air from leaving the area.

Set your ceiling fans to rotate counter-clockwise. You may not know that your ceiling fan needs to be adjusted seasonally. Set to run counter-clockwise in the summer at a higher speed, the fan's airflow will create a wind-chill breeze effect that will make you feel cooler.

Turn on your bathroom fans – or the exhaust fan in your kitchen. Will pull the hot air that rises after you cook or take a steamy shower.

Let the night air in. During summer months temperatures will drop during the night, open the windows to create a wind tunnel/cooling pressure current. If you have the option, open the top section of windows on the downwind side of your house, and open the bottom section of windows on the upwind side.

Get rid of incandescent/traditional lights. Upgrade to LED bulbs as these do not overheat. Incandescent bulbs waste most of their energy in the heat they emit, upgrading to LED will make a small difference in cooling your home while lowering your electric bill.

Cooling units that make no real difference

Air conditioners consume huge amounts of energy and that's adding to climate change. The United States uses as much electricity to keep buildings cool as the whole of Africa (whole Continent) uses for all its electrical needs. That power largely comes from polluting power stations, adding to warmer climate. **The world is set to use more energy for cooling than heating.** With the demand for air

C. B. Hotnoga TMIET AEE BESA

A complete Guide to maximum energy savings in a domestic household

conditioning rising worldwide, it is reckoned than in around 30 years' time more energy could be used for cooling than for heating.

Air conditioning pumps out heat straight into the atmosphere. Like a fridge, it takes heat from the inside of a building or car, then transfers it to the warm outside. That extra heat makes cities hotter, raising night-time temperatures by up to 2C, which then encourages people to turn up their air conditioning even higher.

Extraction and ventilation units

Kitchen extractor fans

Cooker hoods will help eliminate cooking odours from your kitchen. Used to remove grease, fumes, heat and steam, cooker hood are installed above the oven hob and cleanse the air through extraction and re-circulation. Same as any electrical appliance, will use power to run the extraction fan at different speeds and lights above cooker. Unfortunately, many brands will offer deplorable energy ratings. Not intended for a long time in use, please still check energy efficiency before deciding to buy.

Toilet and shower extraction and ventilation

Moisture in a wet room will add to air condensing on colder surfaces, encouraging mould and mildew to grow. An extractor fan will control this condensation and prevent damage and mould, which can cause health problems. Other ways to help keep condensation at bay are to allow plenty of air to circulate throughout your home, so keep windows and doors open as possible; wipe down surfaces and walls to remove excess moisture.

Humidifiers and dehumidifiers

Maintaining the right level of humidity in your home can be a challenge, especially in summer. A humidifier adds moisture to air when it's too dry (below 35% humidity) and a dehumidifier takes moisture out of air when it's too humid (above 50% humidity). A good humidity level for the average home is between 35

41

C. B. Hotnoga TMIET AEE BESA

A complete Guide to maximum energy savings in a domestic household

and 45 percent. Keeping your home humidity level within this range ensures the most comfortable and healthy environment, while also protecting your home from damage caused by excessive dryness and humidity.

A humidifier – increases moisture in the air and is commonly used during winter months when the air is dry. A dehumidifier – decreases moisture in the air and is commonly used during summer months when the air is warm and humid. You can purchase units that are capable of both functions, just remember – the bigger, more powerful and longer time in use – the more expensive they are to run.

Air quality without expense

Usually the most effective way to improve indoor air quality is to eliminate individual sources of pollution or to reduce their emissions. Some sources can be sealed or enclosed; others, like gas stoves, can be adjusted to decrease the amount of missions. In many cases, source control is also a more cost-efficient approach to protecting indoor air quality than increasing ventilation because increasing ventilation can increase energy costs.

Another approach to lowering the concentration of indoor air pollutants in your home is to increase the amount of outdoor air coming indoors. Most home heating and cooling systems, including forced air heating systems, do not mechanically bring fresh air into the house. Opening windows and doors, operating window or loft/attic fans, when the weather permits, or running a window air conditioner with the vent control open, increases the outdoor ventilation rate. Local bathroom or kitchen fans that exhaust outdoors remove contaminants directly from the room where the fan is located and also increase the outdoor ventilation rate.

It is particularly important to take as many of these steps as possible while you are involved in short-term activities that can generate high levels of pollutants: painting, paint stripping, cooking; or engaging in maintenance and hobby activities such as: welding, soldering, sanding. You might also choose to do some of these activities outdoors, if you can and if weather permits.

Ventilation and shading can help control indoor temperatures. Ventilation also helps remove and dilute indoor airborne pollutants coming from

C. B. Hotnoga TMIET AEE BESA

A complete Guide to maximum energy savings in a domestic household

indoor sources. This reduces the level of contaminants and improves indoor air quality. Carefully evaluate using ventilation to reduce indoor air pollutants where there may be outdoor sources of pollutants, such as smoke and refuse, nearby. Natural ventilation describes air movement through open windows and doors. If used properly natural ventilation can at times help moderate the indoor air temperature, which may become too hot in homes without air-conditioning systems or the use of air conditioning is impossible. Natural ventilation can also improve air quality by reducing pollutants that are indoors.

There are many types and sizes of air cleaners on the market, ranging from relatively inexpensive table-top models to sophisticated and expensive whole-house systems. Some air cleaners are highly effective at particle removal, while others, including most table-top models, are much less so. A very efficient collector with low air-circulation rate will not be effective, nor will a cleaner with high air-circulation rate but a less efficient collector. The long-term performance of any air cleaner depends on maintaining it according to the manufacturer's directions.

Miscellaneous electrical consumers

Odd consumer units

Domestic consumer units receive the main electrical supply and distribute it to individual circuits throughout the home to provide electricity. Fuse boxes for homes play a crucial role in helping to prevent electric shocks and electrical fires. A fuse board monitors and detects the current in each circuit and will trip the system if it is being overloaded to protect the premises and its occupants. It is very important they are installed by a qualified professional to ensure that hey are fitted and tested correctly. When considering which product is right for the property, it is important to think about the size of the property, how many circuits are in use and whether a part or fully populated board is required.

Big consumers intended to be used for short periods of time

43

C. B. Hotnoga TMIET AEE BESA

A complete Guide to maximum energy savings in a domestic household

Demand response - in technical terms - is a change in the power consumption of an electric utility customer to better match the demand for power with the utility. In a domestic environment this translates as: you should use home appliances, especially the ones known to use a lot of power, in a better managed way; only for the amount of time they are needed to be in operation and by making the most out of that run time. Such as:

Air conditioners – Dishwashers – Clothes dryers – Drying cabinets – Freezers – Refrigerators – Kitchen stoves – Water heaters – Washing machines – Trash compactors – Microwave ovens – Induction cookers.

Appliances not meant for domestic practice

When looking for energy efficient appliances for your home, you need to look out for the energy ratings label on appliances and consider the size of the appliance you require. Energy ratings are generally given to products based on their size category. This means that two differently sized appliances with the same energy rating may use quite different amounts of electricity. For instance (UK example), an A rated 180-litre fridge freezer could cost only £43 a year to run, whereas a larger 525-litre fridge freezer with a better A+ rating could cost £57 a year to run.

To reduce your energy consumption you have to take control of your electric appliances and avoid leaving such units on standby. The average household will spend 130 pounds/euros/dollars a year powering appliances left in standby mode. This is the energy used by certain appliances when not in use and not switched off at the plug/unplugged. As well as standby power, other new additions to the average household's collection of electrical goods such as broadband modems, broadband routers, digi-boxes and telephones use low levels when not in use. These are not items that we tend to think to turn off, but can gradually go on to consume a great deal of electricity over the year.

Electrical items should be disposed of carefully due to the nature of their materials. Items which have the image of a wheelie bin with a cross on them should not be disposed of using the general household rubbish collection. These items include everything from large white goods to energy saving light bulbs. By keeping waste electrical equipment separate from other waste, the hazardous substances

C. B. Hotnoga TMIET AEE BESA

A complete Guide to maximum energy savings in a domestic household

can be removed and other parts can be recycled rather than sent to landfill. If you are buying new electrical appliances, retailers are obliged by law to either take your old appliances off you for free in store or tell you where you can take your old item for recycling free of charge.

Using commercial or industrial intended consumers on a domestic power supply

Electrical wiring is commonly understood to be an electrical installation for operation by end users within domestic, commercial, industrial, and other buildings, and also in special installations and locations. Installations are distinguished by a number of criteria such as voltage (high, low, extra low), phase (single or 3 phase), nature of electrical signal (power, data) and so forth.

Electrical wiring is ultimately regulated to ensure safety of operation, and there will be Building Regulations in your country that will list "controlled services" such as electrical wiring that must follow specific directions and standards, providing detailed descriptions referred to by legislation. Each country will have a number of specific national practices, habits and traditions that differ significantly from other countries. These include the use of ring circuits (sockets) for domestic fixed wiring, fused plugs and all other "safety related" criteria.

What is to be understood from all this, always follow the letter of the Law in your country, avoid any "contraptions" that might put yourself or others, your property or other people's property at risk. If some piece of machinery will work in your domestic environment, doesn't necessarily mean it is legal, safe or wise to power on and run.

2. Gas supply to your property

Smart gas meters

A smart meter measures your gas and electricity use, just like a traditional meter. We have put the two under separate sections due to different scenarios around the world – some properties might have one but not the other.

45

C. B. Hotnoga TMIET AEE BESA

A complete Guide to maximum energy savings in a domestic household

Unlike a traditional meter, a smart meter sends its readings to your supplier automatically, you won't need to read your gas and electricity meters any more, no more estimated bills. Your bills will be more accurate, automatic meter readings mean they will reflect exactly the energy you use. Will help you keep track of your spending – see what your energy costs in pounds/dollars/euros and pence/cents and set a daily, weekly or monthly budget.

Monitor how much energy you're using – find out which appliances cost the most to run and make small tweaks to your lifestyle to save on bills. Help make energy greener – by using it in a more responsible manner; do your bit to cut carbon emissions. Smart meters work differently, depending on whether they're measuring your electricity or gas, electricity meter is connected to the mains, and monitors how much power you are using in real time. A smart gas meter is battery powered and "asleep" most of the time. It wakes up every half an hour to send a reading via the electricity meter. You might also have an In-Home Display in your home, the smart meter also sends the same information to it so you can monitor your energy usage in real-time and manage how much gas and electricity you use.

Application on gas heating and hot water systems

Gas central heating – if you live in a home that is connected to a gas grid (supply), then it makes sense to assume that a gas-fired central heating system would be the cheapest option for heating your home. In most cases you will already have a gas-fired boiler in your house and you can save money on long-term running costs by opting to install a more reliable and efficient one – either when the one you currently have has failed altogether, or right now; if you have the time and money to spend on buying a new one.

These so-called "wet systems" use a gas-fired boiler that will heat water to provide central heating, usually through radiators or perhaps underfloor heating – and hot water through taps in your home. Because gas is a highly efficient source of fuel, you get a good return for your money on every unit of energy that you use.

C. B. Hotnoga TMIET AEE BESA

A complete Guide to maximum energy savings in a domestic household

Modern condensing gas boilers are now more efficient than ever and by making use of hot flue gases – that is normally wasted in a standard boiler – some newer condensing boilers will operate at around 90% efficiency. Always use a licensed gas engineer when having any gas work carried out in your property – one that holds all the relevant qualifications required for working on your gas-powered appliances and heating systems.

Gas isn't a plentiful natural resource everywhere in the world, many countries are not self-sufficient in its production and having to compete with a growing demand for gas services – like all fossil fuels, it's on the decline because eventually, it will run out. Despite being a popular and regularly used fuel around the world, as a fossil fuel, gas does produce carbon dioxide when being burnt, so can therefore NOT be considered as a clean source of sustainable energy.

Ways to save heat and fuel at home

For most households, energy is an expensive necessity. However, there are a number of things you can do to save heat and fuel at home during winter months, which will not only save you money but will also make your house cosier and sustainable to run.

- Understand your heating system and its controls. Take time to learn how your heating system works – and how to use the controls properly – so that you can use it in the best and most cost-effective way for you. For example: your home will take about 30 minutes to cool down (longer in a well-insulated property) so consider turning the heating off half an hour before you go to bed.

- Turn your thermostat down. Reducing it by 1 degree Celsius could save you energy and money (as much as 100 pounds/dollars/euros per year), without noticing any difference.

- Investigate switching to a different energy supplier. You might be able to get a cheaper deal, especially if you haven't switched for at least three years.

C. B. Hotnoga TMIET AEE BESA

A complete Guide to maximum energy savings in a domestic household

- Avoid drying clothes on your radiators. This lowers the quantity of heat released by the radiators, so the boiler has to run for longer to achieve the same room temperature, thereby using more fuel overall.

- Keep furniture away from radiators. The foam in upholstered furniture is a very effective heat insulator and prevents it getting into your room.

- Use the sun. It's the most readily available source of heat and it's the cheapest. When sunny, make the most of it by opening your internal doors and let the warm air flow through your home.

- Draw the curtains. Especially at night, to keep the warmth in and the cold out. Also, tuck your curtains behind the radiators.

- Fit double or triple glazing. If your windows need replacing, consider fitting either double or triple glazing. Both reduce heat loss through the glass.

- Avoid estimated bills. Keep your bills accurate by submitting regular meter readings to your energy supplier.

- Buy an energy monitor. These allow you to see which appliances use the most electricity so you can adjust how much you use them.

- Time for a new boiler? Install an energy-efficient condensing boiler. These are much more efficient than old boilers.

Gas central heating systems

The basic idea of central heating is really simple: you have a boiler (an easily controllable furnace, fuelled by gas) in a handy place like your kitchen or bathroom and it uses water, moved by an electrically powered pump, to carry heat into radiators in all the other rooms. It's simple, convenient, efficient, and it makes winter days easier to endure.

The boiler is the most important part of a central heating system. It's like a big fire that has a continuous supply of natural gas streaming into it from a pipe

C. B. Hotnoga TMIET AEE BESA

A complete Guide to maximum energy savings in a domestic household

that goes out to a gas main in the street. When you want to heat your home, you switch on the boiler with an electric switch.

We can think of a central heating system as a continuous circuit moving hot water out from the boiler, through all the radiators in turn, and then back again to pick up more heat. In practice, the circuit is usually more complex and convoluted than this. The water is permanently sealed inside the system (unless drained for maintenance); the same water circulates around your home every single day. A thermostat mounted in one room monitors the temperature and switches the boiler off when it's hot enough, switching the boiler back on again when the room gets too cold.

Types of boilers

A central heating system needs to be adequate for your home's needs, without being oversized as this can lead to wasted energy (and of course money). You should consider things like the number of occupants in your property, if you will need to use multiple showers or taps at once and the kind of space available. Fuel type is another big consideration you will need to make when it comes to choosing your home's new heating system. There are plenty of factors that can affect your decision, including your home's connection to gas and power grids, if you want to use renewable energy sources and the kind of space and setup of your property itself.

- Condensing boilers. Typically extract over 90% of the heat from the fuel they burn, making them both cost effective and energy efficient. They offer great value for money over time and also have less of a negative impact on the environment that older boiler types. Whilst they can be a little more expensive to purchase, the fact that they are more energy efficient should outweigh this. Condensing boilers are more complex than some of the older types and therefore maintenance can be a little more costly. The best way to avoid major boiler problems is to have it serviced annually.

- Combi boilers, also known as combination boilers. Are highly efficient and compact, making them ideal for smaller homes. The name Combi comes from the fact that these boilers are able to act as both water heater and also a central

C. B. Hotnoga TMIET AEE BESA

A complete Guide to maximum energy savings in a domestic household

heating unit. They work by heating water directly from the mains, so a hot water storage cylinder or cold-water tank are not needed; this heating method makes them very energy efficient and affordable to run, as water is not heated and stored (and thus wasted if not used). One of the more straightforward boiler to install, also means it tends to be a cheaper option both for installation and repairs. With a combi boiler you cannot run more than one shower or bath at a time (or run a hot tap at the same time), this makes it a less ideal option for larger households with multiple bathrooms. As there is no immersion heater, if your combi boiler breaks down you will not have a backup supply of hot water.

- System boilers. Directly heats your central heating and also produces hot water for your storage cylinder. It is a heat only boiler and works in a similar way to a regular boiler. A hot water storage tank will always be required with a system boiler, as it needs somewhere to store the water it has heated; doesn't require a cold-water tank. It is more straightforward to install than some other boiler types and you can get hot water from multiple sources like taps and showers at the same time without losing water pressure or seeing a temperature drop. Can work with a solar thermal system, which uses the sun's energy to heat water for your home. This can reduce your household's carbon emissions and energy bills. Any hot water created will be kept in a hot water storage tank until it's needed. During this time heat will be lost, so it is important to try and prevent as much of this heat loss as possible by isolating it. You are also limited by the size of your hot water tank, can only use as much hot water as your storage tank can hold; if you require more you must then wait for your boiler to heat it again.

- Regular boilers. The system is made up of a number of parts including a boiler, heating controls, a hot water cylinder, a cold-water storage cistern plus a feed and expansion cistern; can often be found in older, larger homes and less are being installed as time goes by. You can use multiple sources such as taps and showers, without experiencing any effect on water pressure or temperature. These are also compatible with solar thermal panels; do take up a large amount of space – not ideal for smaller homes. You will need to wait for the boiler to heat another tank full before you can use more, so can't have instant hot water. Due to all of its separate parts and pipework, a regular boiler system is one of the more time consuming and costing heating systems to install.

C. B. Hotnoga TMIET AEE BESA

A complete Guide to maximum energy savings in a domestic household

- Gas boilers. There are 3 main types of gas boiler: regular, combi and system. Gas is around 3-4 times cheaper than electricity per kWh making it a much more economical option when it comes to heating your home. Whilst gas is a fossil fuel and therefore not environmentally friendly, it is the cleanest fossil fuel of those available. In fact, gas creates less than half of the CO_2 emissions of oil, and a third of those produced by coal. In order to power a boiler with natural gas you must be connected to the gas network. It can be extremely costly to have your property connected to the grid if it is not already, so in this case you may want to opt for a different fuel type.

Controlling heating in your home

Heating installations vary around the world and also the options to control them. From a basic system, entirely manually controlled – you have to switch it off and on when you feel cold – to electric thermostat that will give you the option of setting the temperature you want and the thermostat switches the boiler on and off to keep the room temperature roughly constant. Most people have heating systems with electronic programmers attached to them that switch the boiler on automatically at certain times of the day (typically, just before they get up in the morning and just before they get in from work).

An alternative way of controlling your boiler is to have a thermostat on the wall in your living room. A thermostat is like a thermometer crossed with an electric switch: when the temperature falls too much, the thermostat activates and switches on an electric circuit; when the temperature rises, the thermostat switches the circuit off. So the thermostat switches the boiler on when the room gets too cold and switches it off again when things are warm enough.

Radiators and heating system around the property

Many people are confused by hot water radiators and think they can operate at different temperatures. A radiator is just a copper pipe bent back and forth 10-12 times or so to create a large surface area through which heat can enter a room. It's either completely on or completely off: by its very nature, it can't be set to different temperatures because hot water is either flowing through it or not.

C. B. Hotnoga TMIET AEE BESA

A complete Guide to maximum energy savings in a domestic household

Thermostatic valves (also known as TRVs) fitted to radiators give you more control over the temperature in individual rooms of your home and help to reduce the energy your boiler uses, saving energy and money. Instead of having all the radiators in your home working equally hard to try to reach same temperature, you can have your living room and bathroom (example) set to be warmer than your bedrooms (or rooms you want to keep cooler).

When the heating first comes on, the boiler fires continuously and any radiators with valves turned on heat rapidly to their maximum temperature. Then, depending on how high you've set the radiator valves, they begin to switch off so the boiler fires less often. That reduces the temperature of the hot water flowing through the radiators and makes them feel somewhat cooler. If the room cools down too much, the valves open up again, increasing the load on the boiler, making it fire up more often, and raising the room temperature once again.

It is not a good idea to fit TRVs in a room where you have your main wall thermostat, because the two will work to oppose one another: if the wall thermostat switches the boiler off, the radiator valve thermostat will try to switch it back on, and vice-versa. If you have adjoining rooms with thermostats set at different temperatures, keep your doors closed; in a cool room with the valve turned down connected to a warm room with the valve turned up, the radiator in the warm room will be working overtime to heat the cool room as well.

Maximizing the efficiency of your heating installation

Install a programable thermostat. What separates a programable thermostat from the others is that they can be programmed to increase or reduce temperatures at pre-determined times based on your schedule. You can automatically adjust the temperature setting to be higher when you're home and lower when you're not, rather than leaving it the higher temperature throughout the day.

Smart and Learning thermostats can interpret the right temperature based on past adjustments and by learning when your home is usually occupied;

52

C. B. Hotnoga TMIET AEE BESA

A complete Guide to maximum energy savings in a domestic household

additionally most of nowadays newer Learning or Smart thermostats can also be connected to some of the more popular home automation systems such as Google Home and Amazon's Alexa. Some of these have the ability to pair with your smartphone to determine when all of the occupants of your home have either left or are returning to the property.

Sealing/Insulating your home can be incredibly beneficial when it comes to maximizing your heating efficiency. The point of sealing your home is to prevent the warm air in your home from escaping, meaning that if you have specific areas in your home where air leaks, you run the risk of losing all the moisture in your home while the cold, dry air enters your house.

Lower your heat. This is not a contradicting way to using your heat, lowering your heat can actually help maximize your heating efficiency. Keeping your heat at a low but constant temperature helps reduce the cost of your bill and prevents your home from overheating 24/7. Instead of setting your thermostat at a high temperature at all times, try putting on an extra layer of clothing to help keep you extra warm without the risk of overheating. Body temperature and "comfort zones" depend a lot on the activities or non-activities we might be performing at the time (example: you might prefer it warmer when sitting on the sofa to watch television but cooler in your bedroom when going to sleep); knowing that you can always go up a couple more degrees on the thermostat if really needed.

Spaces with special heating requirements

Air leaks. Whether you are in a new house or an older one, draft windows, doors and attics allow cold air in and draw heated air out. It is important to seal up any leaks to keep the heat inside. Start by checking the weather-stripping around your windows and doors, and replace if it appears worn; check for any leaks where heated air can "escape" – by sealing air leaks you can make big energy saving on heating – as high as 1/3 less energy used.

Fireplaces. If you have an open fire in your house you will know it can warm a room in a matter of minutes. As a drawback, a fireplace damper left open

C. B. Hotnoga TMIET AEE BESA

A complete Guide to maximum energy savings in a domestic household

when not in use is an invitation for heated air to escape and cold air to funnel into your home. Close the damper after every use and, more important, open it before you light a fire or your home will fill with smoke.

Ceiling fans. Can increase your heating bills as the warm air rises to the top of the room. If you have a ceiling fan, change the direction of the blade during winter; set it to push the air downward along the walls by reversing the flow of the fan. Circulating warm air back through the room will heat the room more evenly and ease the effort your heating source needs to keep the room at a comfortable temperature.

Space heaters. It may seem like a good idea to turn on an electric space heater for a little extra warmth in a small space. It is not, they are expensive to operate, can be dangerous and will cool down sharply after turning off.

Rugs and carpeting. During the cold winter months will add a layer of insultation to the floor, trapping cool air underneath and keeping it from moving up and cooling the room. An extra rug on the floor, or even better – carpeting a room throughout – will make a big difference in controlling the temperature in that space.

Hot water

Controlling the amount of hot water used

Water heating can account for around 12% of a family's utility bill – the biggest chunk after space heating and cooling – you should want to know how to heat your water more efficiently. We can all do something to use less water and save on our bills; no-cost habit changes.

54

C. B. Hotnoga TMIET AEE BESA

A complete Guide to maximum energy savings in a domestic household

Take short showers instead of baths. Your savings here depend on your and your family's habits. A long, hot shower may use a lot more hot water than a bath where the tub isn't fully filled. A warm bath is a nice luxury to relax every now and then, but for daily bathing stick with a shorter shower.

Reduce your time in the shower. Try turning off the water while soaping up, shampooing or shaving. Keep the bathroom and shower cubicle (if you have one) tightly closed, not to get cold, and run the extractor fan to get rid of the steam.

Lower the temperature on the water heater. You can save big.

Don't let the water run needlessly.

Fix leaks. A leak of one drip per second can cost 1 dollar/pound/euro per month. That may not seem like much but, is it more than just dripping?

Install low-flow fixtures/water outlets. Older showerheads and faucets / taps can use more than twice as much water as new ones. For a small investment you can achieve serious savings.

Hot water storage tank

There are two main types of hot water cylinders found in homes today. The newer pressurised unvented hot water tanks and the older style vented hot water tanks.

Unvented hot water cylinders. In an unvented system there is no cold water tank – instead, the sealed hot water cylinder is fed directly by the cold water mains. They offer much better flow rates, meaning your shower and bath

C. B. Hotnoga TMIET AEE BESA

A complete Guide to maximum energy savings in a domestic household

performance should be higher and you don't need to maintain a cold water tank in the loft/attic (which vented systems require). You are not relying on gravity to move hot water around the home so the unvented cylinder can be located pretty much anywhere in your property. Other advantages include reduced noise and since there is no water storage cistern and the system is essentially sealed, the cold water is not at risk from contamination. The major issue with unvented hot water cylinders is that since hot water flow depends on the cold water main pressure; if for any reason the mains water is turned off, your home will be without access to any hot water. These cylinders need to be installed by boiler specialists with relevant qualifications and certifications.

Vented hot water systems. Are still the most common type of hot water system found in many countries. Unlike newer unvented tanks, these are fed by cold water from a storage tank (normally located in the loft/attic) and they use gravity to drive the hot water around the property. The hot water pressure tends to be governed by the height of the water tank above the tap or shower feed. This means that although on the ground floor of the home the pressure might be excellent, in rooms on upper floors the pressure will be lower. As a result, many showers in homes with vented hot water tanks use electric pumps to drive the hot water to the shower at increased pressure. These cylinders are less complicated, simpler to maintain and install, making them a cheaper option.

Controlling when your hot water is needed

Programmers/timers. A timer or programmer allows you to control when your heating and hot water comes on and when it goes off. This is helpful because it means you can programme your central heating to fit around the way your home is used. If you're not at home or are in bed asleep, then the hot water and heating doesn't need to be on. The trick is to set your hot water and heating to come on half an hour before you get home or get up, and set it to switch of half an hour before you no longer need it. This is because an average home takes around 30 minutes to heat up when the heating comes on and 30 minutes to cool down when it goes off.

Setting the hot water timing depends on the type of boiler you have. A Combi boiler only heats up water when you turn on a hot tap, so you don't need to programme it. But if you have a hot water tank, the water tanks will need to be

C. B. Hotnoga TMIET AEE BESA

A complete Guide to maximum energy savings in a domestic household

heated up every now and then during the course of the day. If you need your heating on, the hot water will already be there, if you only need hot water – try an hour in the morning and an hour in the evening; if you don't run out of hot water, that should be enough.

Hot water cylinder thermostats. Hot water tank/cylinder thermostats regulate the temperature of your domestic hot water by switching of the heat supply from your boiler once the set temperature has been reached. They can save you money and avoid wasting energy by over-heating your water. If your hot water tank has its own thermostat, set it to 60 degrees Celsius – hot enough to kill harmful bacteria like Legionella, but not so hot that you're wasting energy. If you find 60 degrees Celsius too hot, mixer taps/faucets can help.

Tap and sink hot water needs

If you look around your house, you'll probably find several taps/faucets. In addition to the kitchen tap, you will find them in the bathrooms: sink, shower and/or bathtub. Not all taps are the same, some may have two handles: one for cold water and one for hot water – others may consist of one handle that you keep turning in one direction to make the water hotter. Water comes out immediately, this is because there is always water running through the plumbing system in your house; it's kept under high pressure. Depending upon exactly what kind of tap you have, different valve-like devices such as mixer taps, single handle mixers, temperature control valves and thermostatic mixing valves – will regulate the temperature of the water before it comes out.

Don't wash or rinse under a running tap; put the plug in the sink first. Fill the sink according to the number of dishes you need to wash – only part fill for a new run or wait until you have enough dishes for a full sink load; you'll use more energy with several small washes than one big one. Use cold or warm water instead of hot and have a second, smaller sink or bowl for rinsing.

Install water efficient tapware or retrofit old tapware.

Bathing requirements

C. B. Hotnoga TMIET AEE BESA

A complete Guide to maximum energy savings in a domestic household

Showers. Take shorter showers, limit time spent in the shower to soap up, wash down and rinse off – will save on energy costs associated with heating water and the price of water itself – use a shower timer. Replace your old shower head with a water saving showerhead. Aerated showerheads reduce the flow but don't compromise on pressure; low flow showerheads reduce the amount of water used, whilst still giving you the feel of a normal shower.

Baths. Only fill the tub with as much water as needed and use less for children. By running your bath just an inch shorter than usual, you can save on average 5 litres of water. Check the temperature as you fill. Adding extra water to get correct temperature after bath is at the right level is wasteful. Regularly check your plug for leaks and replace as necessary.

Brushing your teeth. Remember to turn off the tap while brushing your teeth – a running tap wastes approximately 6 litres per minute.

Where hot water is being wasted

It is difficult to be exact about the energy that is used for heating water because it's hard to measure, and difficult to separate out from the energy your boiler uses for heating. In a typical home the cost of heating water is likely to exceed 10% of total energy bill or approximately a quarter of the fuel used by the boiler; you need hot water all year round, whereas heating is seasonal. The true cost of hot water should also take account of the cost of water itself, which in some cases can be as high as the cost of heating it.

You may be able to reduce the length of time that the water heating is turned on, especially in the summer. Check to see if your power shower has flow controls, if it does you should be able to reduce the flow. With any type of shower, check to see if you can adjust the shower head spray pattern – you may find that you can reduce the flow of water. De-scale your shower heads regularly if you live in a hard water area, otherwise scale build up will affect the water flow. Maintain taps and pipes – leaking or dripping taps and pipes can cost money in wasted water, as well as reduce the efficiency of your hot water system through leakage. It is recommended that you regularly conduct a visual inspection to make sure that there are no leaks or drips.

C. B. Hotnoga TMIET AEE BESA

A complete Guide to maximum energy savings in a domestic household

Gas cooker, hob and oven

Making sure your kitchen appliances are not wasting gas.

You might not necessarily consider the impact that being energy-efficient in the kitchen can have on the bills you pay. This basically comes down to the food you're cooking and the way you're cooking it – being more mindful of your cooking processes can significantly reduce the amount of energy you use and cut your energy bills as you go along.

Cook as much as possible in the oven in one go to make sure all the space and heat is being used. Keep the oven door closed while you're cooking. Each time you open the door, the oven loses heat – as much as 25 degrees – and requires more energy to heat back up to temperature. It's helpful to know how long your oven takes to pre-heat, so you are ready to start cooking as soon as it's up to correct temperature. Use glass or ceramic dishes in the oven; they retain heat better than their metal counterparts, making them the most efficient to use in the oven.

Energy efficiency when cooking will naturally be influenced by the actions you take when preparing every meal, but the appliance you use can also have a bearing on how much energy you use and how expensive your bill is at the end of the month. There is also a question around how much impact an energy-efficient approach to cooking can have on the wider environment; employing better behaviours as much as possible will have a significant effect.

You don't necessarily need to buy a new appliance to ensure energy efficiency when cooking if the one you have works properly. If it isn't working and it's worth replacing – having a cooker in good working order is essential for energy-efficient cooking because it will help lower your fuel consumption and keep your gas and electricity bills down. On electric versions check that your oven thermostat or fan still works, because if air isn't circulating around the interior of the oven, the speed at which food is cooked will be reduced.

Using a gas cooker to its full potential

C. B. Hotnoga TMIET AEE BESA

A complete Guide to maximum energy savings in a domestic household

Hobs tend to be good at simmering: gas hobs offer instant and easy to control heat that tends to spread evenly across the base of your cooking, meaning less time getting your dinner properly cooked. Running costs are lower: gas is cheaper than electricity, so you're likely to save yourself a little money if you cook with this fuel. Gas cookers are known for less-even heat distribution in the oven – you usually won't find fans inside domestic gas ovens, which makes it harder for the heat to circulate evenly around the cavity. This means that a gas oven will usually be hotter at the top than at the bottom. Some people like this temperature gradation, which you can use to your advantage when cooking different dishes at the same time. Hobs can be slow to heat up large volumes: gas hobs are generally slower than electric hobs so you might find yourself hanging around a bit longer to get your dinner going.

Installation: as with any gas-powered appliance, you will need to use the services of a qualified and accredited professional to install a gas or dual-fuel cooker. Dual-fuel freestanding cookers are less common and tent to be a bit more expensive than fully electric or just gas options, but some people like the flexibility they offer. You get the instant heat control of gas for the hob but also the convenience of electrical heat in the oven and grill for more-even heating.

Hob and oven, how not to operate

Cooking is a necessary part of life. For some households as much as 30% of the gas and electricity bill is down to cooking alone. The scale of which depends of your cooking practices.

Use lids on pots and pans. Covering pots and pans helps to trap heat, so you can cook things quicker, or achieve the same level of boiling or frying without having the hob turned up so high.

Use the right size pans. There's no point boiling a small handful of potatoes in a massive pot, you'll just be wasting energy trying to heat up all the excess water. Also, make sure the pan you use is on the correct hob. If you can see any hob area peeking from underneath, you're just losing energy.

60

C. B. Hotnoga TMIET AEE BESA

A complete Guide to maximum energy savings in a domestic household

Cook in batches. Cook as much food in one go as possible, there's no point having the oven on for an hour to cook two dishes separately when they could go in together for 30 minutes. This is especially useful if you're cooking a big meal, or you share a kitchen with others.

Keep your oven and stove top clean. Any bits of burnt food or grease absorb food, making them less efficient.

Switch off the oven early. A decent oven will retain the required temperature for up to 10 minutes after you switch it off, so that is 10 minutes of energy you could save without compromising on your dinner's needs.

Try not to do in your kitchen

Certain cooking habits cause substantial waste of fuel and you can save up to 30% by improving your processes. A couple minutes of planning ensures a big fuel saving. You can avoid an "idle flame" if you prepare and keep all materials and ingredients required for cooking within reach, before lighting the stove. Keeping the flame on the larger burner from burning unnecessarily on a gas stove will amount to a sizeable saving by end of the month.

Use optimum quantity of water. Since water is extensively used in cooking, you should remember that surplus water wastes fuel. By using double the required quantity of water your fuel consumption will increase by 65%.

Reduce the flame when boiling starts. When a vessel's contents reach boiling point, a low flame is enough to keep them boiling. Addition of more heat at the boiling stage causes further evaporation of the liquid without serving any useful purpose. Hence, when water or any other liquid is boiling, reduction in the flame will reduce wastage. You will find that the time taken to cook is just the same but will save 25% fuel.

Shallow, wide vessels save fuel. A visible flame touching the sides of the vessel wastes fuel since it gives out heat to the surroundings. But if you cover the flame as much as possible by using a broad vessel, you will save fuel.

C. B. Hotnoga TMIET AEE BESA

A complete Guide to maximum energy savings in a domestic household

The small burner saves fuel. The lower flame takes a little more time to complete cooking, but then you are not always in such a hurry that you can avoid to save fuel.

Allow frozen food to defrost before cooking. Very cold food consumes a larger amount of energy.

Eating together saves fuel. Frequent reheating of food will not be needed.

3. Insulating your home

Insulation reduces the exchange of heat through a surface such as a wall, attic, duct or roof. In a well-insulated home, less warm air escapes from the house during the winter, and less cool air escapes during the summer, reducing the amount of energy needed for heating and cooling. Improving the insulation in older structures may lower your annual bill by up to 20%.

Floors, walls and attics. The outer shell, or envelope, of your home is the barrier that prevents the temperatures of the inside and outside air from equalizing. The better insulated the walls, floors and roof are, the less energy your heating and cooling systems have to use to warm or cool the air in your home. Since heat rises, insulating your roof is especially important to keep warm air inside in cold climates.

Sealing air leaks. Even walls with good insulation can still let warm or cool air escape through cracks and gaps around windows and doors. Draughty homes require more power to heat and cool than tight homes, so save energy by sealing and weather-proofing to stop air leaks. In older homes, it's virtually impossible to seal the house too tightly; in most cases, because of the construction method used, there will still be enough fresh air to maintain good ventilation after sealing the biggest leaks.

Insulating ducts. In homes with central heating and air-conditioning units that force air through a duct system, leaking ducts may lower efficiency by up to 20 percent. Seal and insulate all ductwork in your house to let the warm and cool air

62

C. B. Hotnoga TMIET AEE BESA

A complete Guide to maximum energy savings in a domestic household

get where it's supposed to go as efficiently as possible. Good insulation is even more important when the ducts travel through unfinished areas like attics and basements. Seal the areas around the registers to keep air from leaking behind the wall or under the floor.

Reflective insulation. While most insulation reduces heat transfer by physically blocking it, reflective insulation – also called a radiant barrier – is installed on the attic floor, where it reflects the heat radiated into the attic by a hot roof and prevents it from entering the living space below. While reflective insulation has some value in lowering heating bills, its main purpose is to keep the house cool in hot climates.

Is your home energy efficient?

Insulating your property will make your home warmer and more comfortable, while also reducing its impact on the environment in the process. Insulation – and draft-proofing – protects your house against cold in winter and excess heat in summer, and can even reduce noise pollution (like the sound from a road or passing aircraft). You should think about insulating the whole "envelope": roof – walls – floor – windows and doors.

Many people make the mistake of assuming that heat only goes up – but only one form of heat transfer primarily moves up. In reality, heat travels in all directions. If you adjoin another home, either through shared walls or through a floor that is in effect another household's ceiling, or vice versa, you are fortunate as you will not suffer from heat loss, assuming the other side is heated as well. However, you will still need to heat your home, as you won't have heat gain either. The general rule is that the bigger the temperature difference, the greater the flow of heat. So, the colder it is outside, the greater the heat loss from your home.

How much heat is being lost from different parts of your home depends on the type of house you live in, whether it's detached or semi-detached, terraced property – mid or end terrace. If you live in a flat, the losses will be different again, and will depend on whether your flat is in the middle, at the top or at ground floor level. For a typical house the walls will lose most heat, around 30% and up to 40%. The roof will be next at around 25%, followed by windows and doors at around 20%,

C. B. Hotnoga TMIET AEE BESA

A complete Guide to maximum energy savings in a domestic household

and the floor (of your lowest storey) at around 10%. Quite a large loss will occur because of draughts and lack of air-tightness.

Good insulation types include many products that typically have a structure similar to wool. In effect a good insulator will trap tiny pockets of air within a material which itself is also a good insulator: mineral and glass wools, sheep's wool, cotton, wood and wood-based products, polystyrene, spray foam and even paper. Good insulation material doesn't just slow the process of heat loss, depending on its specific use, there are other properties that are important too, such as physical strength, fire resistance, resistance to mould, and non-toxicity; cost is another important consideration too.

Unfortunately, many materials with physical strength and which are therefore used in building construction, including metals (copper, steel, aluminium), stone, brick, tiles and concrete, are bad insulators. However, some more modern versions of these materials have been designed to have construction strength but lower heat transmission. Water is also a bad insulator, which means that anything that soaks up moisture will usually conduct heat away quite quickly. Moving air also takes heat away quickly even though air that is prevented from moving, generally when trapped in tiny pockets, makes a good insulator – this principle is used in fabrication of double or triple glazed windows, normally much more efficient nowadays.

Is correct insulation making a difference?

Improving your home's insulation will ensure that you maximize the use of natural resources and don't waste energy. How much money you will save by insulating your home will depend on different factors like the type of insulation and the size of your house. Moreover, depending on how old your house is, you will need to incorporate more or fewer insulation measures. The good thing is that you generally don't need any planning permission for fitting insulation measures and they will eventually pay back so it is a wise investment.

Usually, modern houses are built to good insulation standards, but old houses need a lot of work to be done. In the last case, there are probably many options to improve the energy efficiency of your home. When too cold, heat can be

C. B. Hotnoga TMIET AEE BESA

A complete Guide to maximum energy savings in a domestic household

lost in all directions, so you should think of integral insulation to keep the heat in your house.

Wall insulation. Depending on the type of wall you have, you can use:

-       Cavity wall insulation (there is a gap between the inner and outer leaf). An insulator is inserted into the wall through drilling holes which are then refilled.

-       solid wall insulation (no cavity inside them). If you have solid walls you can choose between internal and external insulation. External insulation normally covers the entire facade of the property while internal is generally applied to inner rooms.

Roof insulation can be:

-       in a warm loft/attic, insulating immediately under the roof. This is more expensive than cold loft but usually a better insulator.

-       in a cold loft/attic, insulating immediately above the ceiling of the top storey/floor.

Window and door insulation. Make sure you have double (or triple) glazed windows and doors. This is, having at least two panels of glass some millimetres apart instead of a single glass. Double glazing will also protect you from outer noise, keeping your home warm and silent.

Floor insulation. This might be very expensive, make sure if you really need it depending on the type of floor you have. Usually, modern houses have insulators under the concrete floor surface, but older builds with suspended floors will need some investment. One very accessible alternative for floor insulation is placing good rugs all around.

Keeping your property warm in the winter and cool in the summer without spending a fortune

C. B. Hotnoga TMIET AEE BESA

A complete Guide to maximum energy savings in a domestic household

In cold climates, heating homes accounts for more than half of household entire energy consumption. So reducing this figure – while keeping homes warm enough – not only cuts energy bills, but helps meet the carbon reduction commitments required in fighting climate change.

Use your curtains. Heat from the sun is free so make the most of it. Open your curtains and let the sunlight in during the day to make use of this free heat. When it gets dark, shut your curtains, which acts as another layer of insulation and keeps warmth in your rooms.

Use timers on your central heating. Programming your boiler to turn the heating on a little earlier – such as 30 minutes before you get up in the morning, but at a lower temperature – is cheaper than turning it on just as you need it at a higher temperature. This is because a boiler heats up at a constant speed, no matter where you set your thermostat. But don't make the mistake of leaving your heating on low all day, because then you're just paying for heat when you don't need it.

Move your furniture. It might feel great to have your favourite seat in front of the radiator, but it's absorbing heat that could be warming your home. By moving it away from the radiator, hot air can circulate freely. The same goes for your curtains or drying clothes – keep them away from the radiator so that you can get the most out of your heat source.

Maximise your insulation. When it comes to heat, around 25% is lost through the roof. This can be easily reduced by installing 25cm of insulation throughout your loft. It's also worth seeing what's going on in your walls, as around a third of the heat in an uninsulated home is lost this way. Another good idea to check with your energy supplier to see if they have any insulation schemes running – which can sometimes mean cheap or free installation.

Wrap up warm. Not just yourself but if you have a hot water tank, make sure it is properly lagged – or insulated. This will keep the water warmer for longer, and reduce heating costs. Insulating an uninsulated water tank could save up to 150 pounds/euros/dollars a year – but even just upgrading your tank's "old jacket" will help to save money.

C. B. Hotnoga TMIET AEE BESA

A complete Guide to maximum energy savings in a domestic household

Turn down the dial. Turning your thermostat down by 1 degree Celsius could cut your heating bill by up to 10%. Keep the dial at 18°C for as much as possible, save money and avoid the negative impact of a cold home.

Block out the draughts. Even a simple solution such as making your own draught excluders will help keep the warmth in your home. Self-adhesive rubber seals around doors and windows and draught excluders are relatively cheap and easy to install. So it is worth getting those doors and windows sealed before winter properly kicks in.

Install thermostatic radiator valves - TRVs. Installing heating controls and thermostatic radiator valves results in energy savings of 40% compared to a house with no controls.

Reflect the heat. Radiator reflector panels are relatively cheap, easy to install and ensure that heat from your radiators warms up your room and not your walls. They work by reflecting the heat back into the room.

Just make the most out of what you already have in place

Connect bathroom exhaust vent switches to same switch as the lights, so vents can't be left on by accident. Vent only when needed. Winter air tends to be dry, so if you don't mind a little less privacy, open your bathroom door and let the steam escape into the house instead.

Make sure bathroom fans/vents have baffles/draft blockers on the outside so you don't have cold air blowing back into the house.

Switch ceiling fans (reverse them) spring and fall. If you have heated floors turn off the ceiling fans; if you have forced air heat, turn them on.

Close the doors and vents in unused room if you are trying to reduce heating costs or keep your living space warmer in an emergency. Be careful not to let rooms get too cold if they have plumbing, so you don't end up with frozen pipes.

C. B. Hotnoga TMIET AEE BESA

A complete Guide to maximum energy savings in a domestic household

Make sure you aren't blocking airflow from forced air vents, and that the vents are open where you need heat. Don't block your vents with furniture or other objects/items.

If you have a fireplace and are not using it, make sure the flue and/or draft are closed. Open chimneys can suck the heat right out of your home, this is one of the biggest issues with open fireplaces – too much heat loss from the room. Consider blocking the chimney with a fireplace insert insulation to reduce heat loss if it will be left unused indefinitely – don't forget to remove if used again.

Insulate hot water/radiator pipes and ductwork running through non-living areas. You don't want that heat dumped in a crawl space or utility area, you want it to get your house warm.

Attic/loft access or attic/loft doors can be the source of large amounts of heat loss. Make sure your attic/loft access is very well insulated.

Don't let the cold radiate up from your floor. Any uninsulated floor can cause more than 10% heat loss in a home. This is especially important if your home is "built on a slab" (no basement). Insulate the floor with warm rugs and/or carpets.

In winter, don't drain a bathtub that is hot. Wait for it to cool before you drain it. If there is a storm coming where you may lose power, fill the tub with hot water. You get additional heat in the home and an emergency water source.

When you finish baking or cooking, leave the stove open slightly to let the home get all that already created heat.

4. Water supply to your property

C. B. Hotnoga TMIET AEE BESA

A complete Guide to maximum energy savings in a domestic household

Water leaks. There is nothing worse than a leak because you are paying for lost water. Make sure to fix all leaks as soon as possible.

Toilets. Account for almost one third of all household water usage. A water efficient dual flush toilet uses about 6 litres on full flush and 4 litres with economy/small flush. This is less than half of a traditional toilet that uses 13 litres per flush. By installing a dual flush toilet, you will make significant water savings.

Showers. The increasing popularity of Power Showers is a significant concern because spending over five minutes in a Power Shower can use more water than taking a bath.

Dishwashers. Washing plates by hand in the kitchen sink accounts for almost 10% of household water consumption. You can save water by installing a water efficient dishwasher that will use the minimal amount of water necessary to clean and rinse. Always wash a full load of dishes for efficiency.

Washing machines. Rating on energy efficiency labels is based on electricity usage and not on water usage. Look for water efficiency as well.

Taps. Buy aerators for each of your household taps. The aerator spreads the stream of water coming out of your tap into tiny droplets. This will prevent splashing and save water by up to 50%.

Garden lawns. Regularly watering your garden lawn with sprinklers can consume a large amount of water.

Plants and flowers. Most plants and flowers require regular watering to grow and stay healthy.

Water butts. Not only save water but collect it as well. Rainwater harvesting by using a water butt in your garden is inexpensive and you will be amazed how much water you can save each year.

Drinking water. Many people waste water by letting the tap run cold before filling up their glass. You can save water by filling a jug or bottle with tap water and keeping this in the fridge; enjoy ice cold water without wasting a drop.

69

C. B. Hotnoga TMIET AEE BESA

A complete Guide to maximum energy savings in a domestic household

Cold water

Water is a precious resource which needs to be used carefully. Water taken from rivers and lakes for human use has an impact on wildlife. By saving water in your home, you can help the environment too.

Flush less water down the toilet. We all probably flush away as much water in a day as we drink in a whole month. Choose a water-saving, low-flush or dual-flush when buying a new toilet.

Switch to showers. A quick shower uses much less water than a bath. Avoid high volume power showers

Use water-efficient appliances. Check label on dishwashers and washing machines for energy efficiency but also the amount of water used per wash.

Fix dripping taps and leaks. Simple plumbing jobs can save a lot of water without being expensive. A new washer costs close to nothing and can be fitted in minutes. You can install a leak detector to warn you about leaks in your house.

Turn off the taps. Collect the cold water that comes through before a tap runs hot and use it for watering plants. Wash fruit and vegetables in a washing up bowl full of water instead of running a tap. Only fill a kettle to the amount needed. Defrost food in the fridge or microwave, not under a running tap.

Make use of greywater and rainwater. Any water that has been used in the home, except water from toilets, is called greywater. Shower, bath and washbasin water can be re-used in the garden. You can also collect rainwater to use in your house for flushing toilets, washing cars, watering plants or even for the washing machine.

Water supply and your provider

C. B. Hotnoga TMIET AEE BESA

A complete Guide to maximum energy savings in a domestic household

If you pay a fixed bill depending on your home's size - without a water meter, your bill will be based on your home's "rateable value". The amount of water used is irrelevant.

If you pay for the water you use – you have a water meter, where the size of your bill depends on your consumption. But as well as water use, water meters usually calculate sewerage bill too. The sewerage costs are higher than everyday water use because of the processing involved in pumping waste water out of your home.

If you do not yet have a water metering system for your property and considering if to get one, the golden rule to remember is: if there are more bedrooms in your house than people, or the same number, check out getting a meter. But then of course, this is the sort of thinking to work out if a meter is financially worthwhile – this is not taking into account being friendly towards the environment. If you are keen on making a difference in the direction of water savings, then it makes sense to also enjoy the results from the financial perspective so – have a water meter installed.

High water usage can force you on to a meter. If you use large amounts of water for non-necessities such as swimming pools, sprinklers or if you live in a water-stressed area, a meter will normally be fitted automatically by your provider/water company. While the water meter billing system is mostly straightforward, it's assumed "what goes in, must come out", and that any water used creates roughly an equivalent amount in sewerage.

Change your habits. For those on a water meter, saving water means saving money. But for those not on meters, it can cut energy bills and help the environment. Nowadays we use an average 150 litres of water a day per person – our grandparents only used around 20. Really makes you think.

C. B. Hotnoga TMIET AEE BESA

A complete Guide to maximum energy savings in a domestic household

Maintenance charges

If you are a small or single occupancy or are actively water conscious, there are many ways, not just to save but also deal and ask you water supplier to "help" towards achieving your goals. You will want to have a water meter installed so you can be in control of how much water you pay for. If you lose water through a leak on pipework beyond the meter you may have to pay for it, some water companies do offer leak detection services. Sometimes it is impractical or too expensive for a water company to fit a meter because, for example, the work involves separating the pipework in a tower block.

You are normally responsible for repairing water leaks inside your property and in external pipes up to the boundary of your property. Some, not all, water companies offer free repair services for external leaks. If a leak is in your supply pipe and not covered by a water company's free repair service, you are responsible for repairing it. If the leak is not repaired within a certain time, the water company may carry out the repair and charge you for the work.

Compulsory metering water companies are legally entitled to install meters in areas that have been declared as being seriously water stressed. Customers in these areas, are being switched over to water meters and if you live in one of these areas you will have no choice on how you are charged. Your water company can insist you have a water meter installed if you have a swimming pool, power shower, large bath or garden sprinkler. Surface water is the rainwater that drains from a property into a sewer. The water company collect and treats this water and charges customers for the service.

Temporary water use restriction – if there has been a prolonged period of low rainfall, it may become necessary for the water companies to take steps to ensure supplies are maintained and the natural water sources they rely on are conserved. Companies may impose different levels of restrictions on water use depending on the severity of the situation. Draught orders give a water company the power to ban all non-essential use. Draught permits allow companies to take water temporarily from other sources such as rivers and groundwater. Emergency draught orders allow companies to restrict water use in any way deemed necessary, which could, in a very severe drought, mean cutting off water supply to homes and setting

C. B. Hotnoga TMIET AEE BESA

A complete Guide to maximum energy savings in a domestic household

up standpipes in streets. Being water efficient is important at all times but during a drought situation, it helps to conserve limited resources and avoid more severe restrictions becoming necessary.

Where water is lost

Saving water saves money. Installing simple devices such as water-efficient taps and showers will save both water and energy by minimising the use of heated water. About 20% of a typical gas heated home's heating bill is from the water for showers, bath and the hot water tap. Such large financial savings can be particularly vital for households facing water and energy poverty.

Our use of water and energy are closely linked. Operational emissions from the water industry will account in carbon emissions. This is because water treatment is energy and chemical intensive and transporting water around all parts of the world requires a great deal of pumping. Reducing your water use will therefore have an impact on your carbon footprint.

Using water efficiently means that we can minimise the amount of additional water resources being taken out of our rivers and aquifers, especially as demands are rising. This protects our water resources and the wildlife that live in and use them too.

As water resources become more scarce building new infrastructure to meet growing demand becomes increasingly expensive. If we save water instead, we can offset the need for new infrastructure and reduce pressure on existing ones. Additionally, efficient water use makes our supply more resilient against impacts from climate change, such as droughts.

Home appliances that use cold water

A great many households are already making savings and making a difference – engaging in water saving behaviours, cutting their bills and conserving resources. But since the average home uses nearly 350 litres of water every day, there is still astonishing potential to save water, energy and utility bills through further change.

C. B. Hotnoga TMIET AEE BESA

A complete Guide to maximum energy savings in a domestic household

Simplest actions can mean the biggest savings. The key to success is to ramp up consumer engagement, educate families more about water and energy, and offer household specific solutions for reducing bills. Energy and water bills are on the rise, and there is increasing pressure on our natural resources. A new approach is needed to help people get control of water and energy used in the home.

Washing machine

The water efficiency of washing machines can vary greatly. The most efficient washing machine will use 6 litres of water per kilogram of clothing in comparison to the least efficient washing machine that will use 14 litres of water per kilogram. Checking the water consumption box on the energy label will help you to identify if your appliance is efficient or not.

Only wash full loads. Washing machines operate at maximum efficiency when the drum is full. If you tend not to fill the drum you should wash less frequently or consider buying a washing machine with a smaller drum.

Use cotton wash instead of synthetic wash. To avoid creasing, synthetic wash programmes use 50% more water than cotton washes.

Do not use extra rinse. If your washing programme is set to use extra rinse, this will obviously use more water than necessary. The purpose of extra rinse is to ensure the fabric softener is completely removed for the benefit of people with sensitive skin.

When buying a new washing machine, check the water efficiency label.

Dishwasher

Save water with an energy save or eco program. Energy-save or eco programs wash your items at a lower temperature and use less water during each cycle. That will help you save water and cut energy costs, as well as money on your water bill if you're on a water meter.

C. B. Hotnoga TMIET AEE BESA

A complete Guide to maximum energy savings in a domestic household

Go for the full load. Before running the dishwasher wait until you have a full load to ensure that the device is at maximum capacity before you switch it on. This will help make the most of the energy, water and detergent the dishwasher uses.

Skip the pre-rinse. Save water by avoiding rinsing the plates under the tap before placing them in the dishwasher or by using a dishwasher pre-rinse program. Most dishwashers today are powerful enough to get all the dirt off, so a lot of pre-rinsing by hand is often just a waste of water and time.

Turn down the heat. Most modern dishwashers have booster heaters to heat the water that comes from your home's supply. Turning the thermostat down on your hot water will result in additional energy saving without compromising on cleanliness.

Choose your dishwasher wisely. Look for a dishwasher that is rated for energy and water efficiency. Choose the size model that fits your needs. A compact model is more efficient than a large one unless you have to run it several times a day. Using fewer dishes and utensils over the course of the day means doing less washing cycles in the dishwasher, saving water, energy, and detergent.

Water dispensing units

As pollution and water shortages are more and more visible issues, it is not always easy to have access to proper, pure drinking water. Water dispensers, whatever their type or model, are today more and more used in private homes as well. They supply filtered drinking water, connected straight from your water mains or, some people even preferring to have bottled water delivered to their door.

Water dispensers and water coolers haven't necessarily got to be purchased, some people prefer renting or leasing. Buying your water dispenser means you have to consider the costs of accessories, service and maintenance in addition to the water cooler price itself.

C. B. Hotnoga TMIET AEE BESA

A complete Guide to maximum energy savings in a domestic household

Plumbed-in dispensers are mains fed water coolers and normally a little more expensive than bottled water coolers (where you have to pay for bottled water to be delivered to you by a supplier). Some water dispensers are more technologically advanced, but also more expensive to buy and run, can provide: hot, cold and even sparkling water.

If you use such a system in your home or thinking about getting one, should also consider other related costs, such as: maintenance, cleaning and sanitization, replacement parts.

Special taps

When choosing taps for a kitchen or bathroom it's best to consider your options carefully and opt for the best possible tap for the job, to get the efficiency and performance you require.

Pull out rinse taps. With this option, you can use pull out rinser (the spout) of the tap to make full use of your kitchen sink and enjoy more flexibility whilst targeting otherwise difficult to reach parts. Most pull out rinser taps have an aerator for champagne-style flow and are suitable for single and multiple bowl sinks.

Filtered taps. If you have big concerns about the purity of your water, filter taps are designed to remove impurities whilst ensuring you don't need to miss out on the minerals that benefit you and can enjoy water of a normal taste.

Kettle taps. Are also known as instant hot water taps and mean you no longer need to boil your kettle to get water to the required temperature. Kettle taps are a little more energy-efficient and reliable than they were in the past. Have become increasingly popular over recent years and it is claimed that heating water in this way is more affordable and eco-friendly than using a kettle because of the reduced waste involved. Good quality, efficiency and reliability makes are unfortunately expensive.

Cold bathing and washing water

Water usage around the home can be categorised as both direct and indirect. Direct water usage is conscious use of water around the home, be that

76

C. B. Hotnoga TMIET AEE BESA

A complete Guide to maximum energy savings in a domestic household

turning the tap on or taking a shower. Indirect water usage is the water needed to produce the goods or services that we buy on day to day basis. Whilst it can be difficult to lower our indirect water usage, reducing the amount of water we consume in the home can be a simple task.

Water is precious. Those who economise with it can help to reduce the impact on the environment – as well as their wallets. Saving water is easy. Even making small changes to your everyday habits can help. In many parts of the world, every drop counts. You can save precious water too.

Take a shower instead of a bath: this saves a huge amount of water. A warm bath consumes 100 to 200 litres of water, depending on the size of the bath. This is quite a lot, especially since every litre needs to be heated up. Showering is considerably more economical: this consumes just 40 to 60 litres on average.

Use eco-smart showers, you can save up to 60% water compared to traditional shower heads. Less water needs to be heated so you save energy too.

Use air to add effervescence and aeration to the water. Less shower water doesn't mean less showering comfort. Shower heads with this function will offer the same feeling in a more environmentally friendly shower.

In our bathrooms and kitchens, water often disappears down the drain unused – solely because old-fashioned taps or outdated shower systems allow it to drain away.

If you don't have any solar collectors on the roof and don't use any geothermal energy, then you invariably consume fossil fuels for your hot water provision. If you can manage to save water on a daily basis, you will reduce climate damaging carbon dioxide emissions and therefore your carbon footprint too. Plus, you will also reduce your energy bill.

Bath water

Baths have always had a bad reputation and the advice is to take showers rather than baths. However, if you have a power shower (using more than a bath), take long showers, or have kids and might actually be better of having a bath: fill up

C. B. Hotnoga TMIET AEE BESA

A complete Guide to maximum energy savings in a domestic household

with less water – bath the kids together or one after the other using the same water (maybe with a small top up of hot if getting cooler) – leave the bath water in the tub and use it to flush the toilet for the rest of the day.

Showering

A standard 5-minute shower can use about 35 litres of water. By running a power shower, you can be using anything up to 125 litres. If you're not willing to give up any of your showering time, then you could always install a water saving shower head. For regular bath dwellers, it might be a good idea to mix it up a little and opt for a shower every now and then.

Toilet sinks

We are all a bit guilty of leaving the tap running without good reason. In reality our brief moment can cause as much as 10 litres per minute of water wastage. It's not just running taps that can be a problem within the bathroom. Leaking taps are also a huge contributor to water waste around the home.

Flushing toilets

Around a third of all water usage in the average household is flushed down the toilet. A lot of the time, the culprit is an old cistern with a high flush capacity that uses a lot more water than is necessary. Newer cisterns will offer a dual flush system, allowing much more control over the water used with each flush. In times of hardship you can take it as far as: "If it's yellow, let it mellow. If it's brown, flush it down". The idea is not to flush the toilet each time you just do a wee.

Sometimes, old cisterns can be leaking water without you ever knowing it. The quickest way to determine if you have a leaking cistern is to add a little food colouring into the tank. If you see any coloured water running down the pan without you ever having pushed the flusher, then you may well have a crack or a leak.

C. B. Hotnoga TMIET AEE BESA

A complete Guide to maximum energy savings in a domestic household

Hot water

Water used in your heating system

Nobody ever wants to pay more than is necessary for household utilities. Everyone should be motivated to save money wherever possible to get the most out of the home budget. During the colder months, heating costs are a particularly big part of your monthly outgoings, so it may be helpful to identify ways to save money on heating bills that are easy to implement.

Think about when you actually need the heating. For instance, there's no point heating the house when everyone is out at work/school. Choose set times when you want the home to be homely, and periodically review whether these times can be shortened without anyone noticing.

Learn to be financially responsible. Learning to save money on heating bills may be an important part of your household budgeting skills, but perhaps other areas could also do with some attention. Effective budgeting is essential for making the most of the household income but not everyone has the financial discipline to spend wisely. Set some time aside to examine your general behaviour around money and review your spending habits in detail. You'll be amazed at the savings you'll be able to identify if you really put your mind to it.

Bathing hot water

Lower the level of your normal bath by a couple of centimetres.

Replace one or a few of your weekly baths with a short shower.

Showering

Try the four-minute shower challenge or try to take a minute less.

Fit a water efficient shower head or flow regulator.

C. B. Hotnoga TMIET AEE BESA

A complete Guide to maximum energy savings in a domestic household

Hot water and kitchen sink

Block the sink or use a washing up bowl rather than running the tap.

Add a tap aerator to reduce water flow but maintain pressure.

Hot water and toilet sinks

Turn the tap off when brushing your teeth, washing or shaving.

Fit a tap aerator to reduce water flow but keep same pressure.

Water used in large amounts

With a water meter, if you use less water, less often, you keep more money in your pocket. No meter? You can still save on your energy bills if you use less hot water.

- Fit water-saving widgets

- Fix the flush

- Don't let it leak

Gardening / watering

It's important to save water in the garden for two reasons. First, to save money if you are on a water meter. Second, because at peak demand up to 70% of our water supply can be used in gardens, which forces suppliers to use groundwater and take it from streams. This can cause environmental damage and increase water prices.

C. B. Hotnoga TMIET AEE BESA

A complete Guide to maximum energy savings in a domestic household

Water at the right time and use the right amount of water. Many of us over-water our gardens. This is not only wasteful, it means we're doing more work than we need to. Watering the garden before a drought sets in keeps the soil's moisture levels up and helps prevent a water deficit. You should also water plants in the evening when it's cooler to reduce evaporation.

Collect rainwater and reuse old water. It's simple to collect rainwater: just divert the water from your drainpipe into a water but or any other sort of a tank. Reusing greywater (water from baths, showers, washing machines and washing up) is a good way to use water a second time. You can install greywater diverters that divert the water from your bath to an irrigation system or a water but. Household soaps and detergents are harmless to plants but don't use water containing bleach, disinfectant, dishwater salt or stronger cleaners.

Washing vehicles and cleaning jobs

With draught affecting large areas of the world on a growing basis, it is more important than ever to conserve water. This includes saving water while performing everyday tasks such as washing your vehicle. Whether you want to use less water, or no water at all, you can save on your water consumption while still maintaining same "standards".

Using no water. Is one great way to wash your vehicle that uses no water at all, involves using a waterless car wash cleaner. For a quick job when your vehicle is not extremely dirty, there is plenty of option in products out there.

Using less water. You avoid spraying water on your vehicle with a hose and use a bucket of water (or two buckets to keep a cleaner and dirtier rinsing option) and sponge to wipe down the vehicle.

Pools

If you have your own swimming pool, getting smart, water-smart in reducing and control of water loses – will save you big. It is not about just water, but water heated to a certain temperature and all equipment to keep it running, safe and comfortable for bathing.

C. B. Hotnoga TMIET AEE BESA

A complete Guide to maximum energy savings in a domestic household

Use a pool cover. Without a swimming pool cover more than half the water in your pool can evaporate in one year. Using a cover regularly reduces evaporation by 90 to 95%. Will reduce the need to use more chemicals, algae growth and conserve heat, with will save money on heating costs.

Check for leaks. Look for damp spots downstream of the pool, check for leaking pipes, valves and joiners. Loose tiles or cracks can also be an indicator.

Lower the pool's water level. Besides conserving water, keeping a lower water level in the pool helps reduce water loss from extreme splashing.

Lower the temperature on heated pools. If you have a pool heater, reduce the temperature during the summer. Will reduce the occurrence to water loss to evaporation and is especially important when pool isn't being used.

Backwash pool filters only when necessary. Backwashing filters uses extra water so keep the pool clean to reduce the frequency of this being needed. Reuse backwash and dechlorinated waste pool water on lawns and shrubs or collect it to reuse.

Monitor your water and utility bills. Any changes might signal a possible leak or other problem that will need further investigation.

Drain your pool only when absolutely necessary. If a pool has been properly maintained, it may not have to be drained completely or as frequently as you might assume.

Check the pool pump. Run the pump only as long as needed. Start by running the pump for 8 hours per day. If the pool stays clear, run the pump less often. If it starts to get cloudy, run it a bit more each day until it clears. You can also save on operating costs by matching the size of the pump to the needs of your pool.

Hot tubs and outdoor showers

Leave your heater activated between uses. Leaving the heater activated all of the time, if using a spa regularly – say 3 or more times per week. Set water temperature to 3-4°C less than desired bathing set-point and then an hour or two

C. B. Hotnoga TMIET AEE BESA

A complete Guide to maximum energy savings in a domestic household

before using, nudge it up to where you want it to be. This is better than letting the temperature rise and fall a great amount, which uses more energy each time.

Make the most of your lid/cover. One of the most common causes of temperature loss is a damaged, insecure or un-inflated lid or simply not using it at all. Heat always rises so any holes, rips or gaps in the lid can dramatically impact water temperature.

Locate your spa/hot tub near a natural windbreak. Will help maintain a steady water temperature. Wind exposure reduces temperature and something as simple as fencing or a dome forms an effective shield.

Insulate and protect the bottom of your spa. Keeping the underside insulated is a great way to reduce running costs and protect your hot tub. A floor protector not only helps stop heat from dispersing as rapidly when it comes into contact with colder surfaces, but it can also help increase the lifespan of your spa against abrasions and other damage.

Make use of your power saving timer – if one is present. The power saving timer is ideal for ensuring your spa is as cost efficient as possible. It prevents wastage of power by allowing you to set the time and duration of the heating cycle for the spa so that you can enjoy your spa at a time of your choosing, without having to leave the heater on at all times.

Fill from the warm tap. A simple but effective way to save money when filling your spa is to use water from the hot tap. It is usually cheaper to start your spa with warm water (ensure the water is no hotter than 40°C) rather than filling with cold water and waiting for the spa to heat up itself.

End review and guidance

This guide is by no means "set in stone". You have to identify what works for you and your property. So many ideas have been given above, it is only a matter of making more conscious, smarter choices and the occasional adjustment. Can totally understand and appreciate that going through this whole read in one go

C. B. Hotnoga TMIET AEE BESA

A complete Guide to maximum energy savings in a domestic household

might feel like homework, more work, or just another burden. It is not; you now have the information and the way you decide to put it to good use is in your hands. Give it time.

The hardest part, for most people, is changing the routine, making that small change in habits and having to give a second thought to things they have never taken into consideration before. Do it for the satisfaction of checking your monthly supplier bill against the same from last year and seeing the difference, enjoy the savings.

None of this has anything to do with reducing or cutting down on the things you love, taking a bath or forgetting to switch something off. Be more aware of what you are buying in the first place, energy rating and efficiency, if you really need that item. Energy savings start with better controlling home appliances you already have and understanding that if not checked every now and then, will keep on consuming as that is what they've been manufactured to do, so many even after being switched off.

When away from home for a longer period of time, remember to unplug: TV boxes, Internet devices, chargers and anything else not needed with a potential of still running in OFF mode. Also switch off or turn all the way down: heating system, air conditioning, hot water, fridge/freezer, hot/cold drinking water dispensers, fans, lights that are not needed. In exactly the same way all these devices are purchased, brought into our homes, installed and set up to run, they will also need to be told when not needed. And that is under your control.

C. B. Hotnoga TMIET AEE BESA